Y

G ... rsity
o ... an
U

Sean O'Casey

THE SHADOW OF A GUNMAN

Notes by Patrick Rafroidi

AGRÉGÉ D'ANGLAIS, DOCTEUR-ÈS-LETTRES (SORBONNE)
Professor of English and Anglo-Irish Literature, University of Lille

LONGMAN
YORK PRESS

Extracts from *The Shadow of a Gunman* by Sean O'Casey are reprinted by kind permission of Macmillan Publishers Ltd, London and Basingstoke, and St Martin's Press, Inc., New York.

Extracts from *Inishfallen, Fare Thee Well (Autobiographies)* by Sean O'Casey are reprinted by kind permission of Macmillan Publishers Ltd, London and Basingstoke, and Macmillan Publishing Co., Inc., New York. Copyright 1949 by Sean O'Casey, renewed 1977 by Eileen O'Casey, Breon O'Casey, and Shivaun O'Casey.

YORK PRESS
Immeuble Esseily, Place Riad Solh, Beirut.

LONGMAN GROUP LIMITED
Burnt Mill,
Harlow, Essex

First published 1983
ISBN 0 582 78232 5
Printed in Hong Kong by
Wilture Enterprises (International) Ltd.

Contents

Part 1

Introduction

The life and works of Sean O'Casey

The playwright was born John Casey in Dublin on 30 March 1880, the youngest of a large Protestant family of thirteen children of which five survived childhood.

His father died in 1886 and the Caseys, who had not been very well-to-do before, now had to live in progressively poorer tenements, John's mother finding it harder and harder to make ends meet and the boy's life being further embittered by trachoma, a serious disease of the eyes which not only caused constant pain but prevented him from attending school regularly or playing with other children.

In 1891, at the age of eleven, he accompanied his brother Archie to the Queen's Theatre, Dublin, and was thus introduced to the dramas of Shakespeare and Dion Boucicault (in whose play *The Shaughraun* he was to play as understudy for the part of Father Dolan in 1895). His sister taught him to read and he began making up for his lack of formal education.

In 1894, at the age of fourteen, he started work in the stockroom of a hardware store. This was the first of many jobs, clerical and manual, the longest of which was as labourer on the Great Northern Railway of Ireland from 1901 to 1911. In *Red Roses for Me* he would remember the strike that took place there in the latter year.

From 1906 to 1914, he joined a number of nationalist or revolutionary societies: the Gaelic League, founded in 1893 to foster the original language and literature, which truly proved his university (it was then he learnt Irish and gaelicised his name to Sean O'Cathasaigh—later partly to re-anglicise it to Sean O'Casey); the Saint Laurence O'Toole Club and its Irish Pipers' Band; the Irish Citizen Army, of which he became secretary early in 1914, being responsible for drawing up its new Constitution which was endorsed in March of that year. However, he was to resign on 17 July 1914 in opposition to the ICA's too close ties with the Irish Volunteers, an organisation more nationalist than socialist with several anti-labour men in its ranks.

In 1907 his first published work appeared, an article on the Irish educational system in *The Peasant and Irish Ireland*; this was followed in 1917 by *The Story of Thomas Ashe* and *Lament for Thomas Ashe* (he was a member of the ICA who had recently died on hunger strike);

in 1918 by *Songs of the Wren* (1 and 2) and *More Songs of the Wren*, and in 1919 by *The Story of the Irish Citizen Army*. He had also tried his hand at drama but his first play, *The Frost in the Flower*, written in 1911 for an amateur group, was judged too satirical, and the Abbey Theatre also rejected it in 1919 as well as, in 1920, *The Harvest Festival* and *The Crimson in the Tri-Colour*. Only the second play has survived.

Meanwhile some of the most important personal and national events that were to shape O'Casey's life were happening: the deaths of his sister Isabella and his mother in 1918; the 1916 revolution (the background to *The Plough and the Stars*) and the execution of its leaders; the subsequent War of Independence lasting from 1917 to 1921, with guerrilla operations by the Irish Republican Army (successor to the previous bodies that had been banned) against British troops and counter-terrorist forces such as the Black and Tans (the background to *The Shadow of a Gunman*); the signing on 6 December 1921 of a Peace Treaty with England which divided the country between its partisans (Freestaters) and opponents (Republicans) and launched the Civil War of 1922–3 (the background to *Juno and the Paycock*).

In 1923 Sean O'Casey, whose earliest desire had been to have a play staged at the Abbey, saw his dream come true at long last with the production of *The Shadow of a Gunman*—a popular and critical success, and *Kathleen Listens In*, which was coldly received.

In 1924 *Juno and the Paycock* (first staged on 3 March) became the most successful play in the Abbey's twenty-year history, before beginning a long London run in November of the following year. This was followed (also in 1924) by *Nannie's Night Out*, a one-act farce.

On 8 February 1926 *The Plough and the Stars* opened to the accompaniment of riots, and a much protracted controversy followed. A month later, O'Casey visited London to receive the Hawthornden Prize for *Juno and the Paycock*, and settled in England, where he was to live in self-imposed and often bitter exile for the rest of his life.

On 23 September 1927 O'Casey married Eileen Carey Reynolds, a young Irish actress. A son, Breon, was born in 1928, the year when the Abbey Theatre rejected the author's superb experimental play on the First World War, *The Silver Tassie*; it was staged at the Apollo Theatre, London, on 11 October 1929. The rejection was one of the reasons for O'Casey's refusal, in 1932, to become a founder member of the Irish Academy of Letters on W.B. Yeats's (1865–1939) and G.B. Shaw's (1856–1950) invitation, even though Ireland remains in the centre of several of his subsequent plays: for instance, *A Pound on Demand* (1934), a one-act comedy in Irish dialect about two drunks in a post office; the two works with a Dublin strike setting, *The Star Turns Red* (1940), whose hero 'Red Jim', modelled on the Irish labour leader James Larkin, represents the virtues of Communism, and *Red*

Roses for Me (1942–3); the four satirical comedies of rural Ireland: *Purple Dust* (1943), in which two pompous Englishmen try to restore an old mansion in an Irish village in spite of the opposition of nature (a flood) and of comic Irish peasants; *Cock-a-Doodle Dandy* (1949), where a man-size farmyard bird embodies the forces of life and joy against puritanism; *The Bishop's Bonfire* (1955), about preparations for a prelate's visit; *The Drums of Father Ned* (1958), commissioned for the Dublin Festival, to which the Catholic Archbishop objected, leading O'Casey and his fellow Irish author Samuel Beckett (*b*. 1906) to withdraw their works. (The play was first performed in America the following year.)

In 1933 O'Casey's play with a London setting, *Within the Gates*, was published; in 1934 he went to the United States to see it staged in New York; also in 1934 there appeared *Windfalls*, a collection of early poems, short stories and one-act plays (including *The End of the Beginning*).

In 1935 his son Niall was born. He was later to die of leukemia in 1956. In 1937 the miscellaneous collection *The Flying Wasp* was published; it gives a good idea of O'Casey's views on drama. In 1938 he settled in Devon, and the following year a daughter, Shivaun, was born; also in that year, Macmillan issued the first volume of O'Casey's controversial *Autobiographies*. It was called *I Knock at the Door*, and covered the period 1880–90. The sequence was to be completed by five further volumes: in 1942, *Pictures in the Hallway* (covering 1891–1904); in 1945, *Drums Under the Windows* (1905–16); in 1949, *Inishfallen, Fare Thee Well* (1916–26, including therefore the years when *The Shadow of a Gunman* was conceived and produced); in 1952, *Rose and Crown* (1926–34); in 1954, *Sunset and Evening Star* (1934–53).

In 1947 the first performance of *Oak Leaves and Lavender*, set against the background of the Battle of Britain in the Second World War, was given in London. (It had been staged in Swedish, at Hälsingborg, the year before.)

In 1952 three short plays by O'Casey were performed in New York: *Bedtime Story*, *Hall of Healing* and *Time to Go*. They open the author's last period of production which includes, in 1956, *The Green Crow* (miscellaneous); in 1961–2, three more short plays: *Behind the Green Curtains*, *Figuro in the Night* and *The Moon Shines on Kylenamoe*; in 1962, *Feathers from the Green Crow*, a collection of miscellaneous writings as was *Under a Colored Cap* (1963), and the posthumous *Blasts and Benedictions* (1967), whose title aptly describes O'Casey's duality of moods and attitudes.

In 1960 the year of his eightieth birthday, he refused several distinctions, including a CBE and various honorary degrees. He died in Torquay of a heart attack on 18 September 1964.

The historical background of the play

It is, obviously, the contemporary background that plays the most important part in Sean O'Casey's early works: the efforts of the unions in *The Harvest Festival*, the latent antagonism between Labour and nationalist Sinn Fein in *The Crimson in the Tri-Colour*, the main episodes of the struggle for liberation in the Dublin trilogy, the 1916 revolution in *The Plough and the Stars*, the 'War of Independence' in *The Shadow of a Gunman*, the ensuing Civil War in *Juno and the Paycock*.

Such events, however, were the consequence of a long history and they were lived, besides, by a people with a nearly morbid preoccupation with the past. In order properly to understand some of the references and allusions in a play by O'Casey, a backward glance is therefore necessary.

The earliest period referred to in *The Shadow of a Gunman* is the late seventeenth century, with the famous and decisive Battle of the Boyne, in 1690, although there is a hint of a much more distant time, when the Gaels ruled over Ireland. Those Gaels, who arrived in the country some time between the sixth and the first century BC, and were to reach such a state of flowering civilisation as to earn for Ireland, after they had become Christians in the sixth century AD, the title of 'Land of Saints and Scholars', had themselves replaced more or less mythical inhabitants, some of whom are mentioned in O'Casey's play. These were the heroes of oral tales such as those in the so-called Mythological Cycle which includes such figures as Balor of the Evil Eye, the King of the Fomors. Their deeds were extolled in their turn in the Ulster (or Heroic, or Red Branch) Cycle, whose main hero is Cuchulain; in the Fenian or Ossianic Cycle, that told of Finn and his warriors; in the Historical Cycle; and in the poetry of their highly trained poets (the *filid*) and bards, members of a caste who appeared all the more fearful because their satire (when they turned to it instead of indulging in panegyrics) was supposed to be capable of, literally, killing.

The first invaders of Gaelic Ireland, the Vikings (from 795 to 1014) and the Anglo-Normans (from 1169) were assimilated, and added to the wealth and the reputation of the country. With the Anglo-Normans, however, England set foot in the neighbouring island and, from the Renaissance onwards, strengthened her hold and gradually turned into a colony a country which remained faithful to different traditions, a different language, and even a different religion: the bulk of the native Irish refused to abandon Catholicism for Protestantism, England's official creed from the time of Henry VIII.

The English finally succeeded, in parts, in eradicating traditions and even language; they utterly failed in their attempt against religion, in spite of the various 'planters', or settlers, whom they imported, and the sanguinary exactions of a leader like Cromwell. Yet they managed, politically and socially, to crush the Catholics who had taken the side of James II against William of Orange and were subjected after the Treaty of Limerick (1691) to 'penal laws' that took away all legal existence from them until the Catholic Emancipation Act of 1829. But this policy only enhanced the power of the Roman Church in Ireland, which became identified with the struggle for national recognition in spite of the conservative nature of its hierarchy; the very excesses of such a policy finally won over to the Irish cause many members of the recently established Anglo-Irish Protestant Ascendancy and even some Scotch Presbyterians from the North.

'Many a true Irishman was a Protestant', the Roman Catholic Seumas remarks to the 'Orangeman' Grigson in Act II of *The Shadow of a Gunman*, and he calls on the names of Tone, Emmet and Parnell. His list is correct, though incomplete: he might have mentioned Swift, who fought for Irish trade and Irish currency, Grattan, who was responsible for the existence of the short-lived Irish independent Parliament (1783–1800), and several others. But Theobald Wolfe Tone (1763–98), who tried to do away with the religious divisions of the country (he was one of the founders of the Society of United Irishmen) and advocated physical force for its liberation from an alien power, was indeed a significant figure, even though he was too much of a revolutionary in the French 1789 sense of the word to gain sufficient support from royalist Anglo-Irish settlers or anti-secular Catholics. The rebellion he led in 1798 ended in cruel repression and his own death, besides giving 'unionists' a good opportunity to become one again with Britain (this is what occurred in the Act of Union of 1800) and strengthening Protestant extremists in their opposition to what they would later call 'Rome Rule'. Robert Emmet (1778–1803) was also important, albeit in a different way, in showing, by his abortive attempt to seize Dublin Castle (the headquarters of the English Viceroy who ruled Ireland), the symbolic value of self-sacrifice—a lesson that was not lost on the leader of the 1916 revolution, Patrick Pearse (1879–1916). As for Charles Stewart Parnell (1846–91), he represents yet a third aspect of the fight: parliamentary struggle, in a peaceful, legal form of action that might have spared Ireland the atrocities that were to come if his own influence had not been sapped by certain aspects of his private life which were exploited against him, and if the British Government had not kept postponing reforms and Home Rule at a time when the Irish were no longer prepared to wait.

Cultural elements played no insignificant part in the growth of such impatience. A nationalist revival, to which O'Casey was no stranger, swept over the country in the late nineteenth and early twentieth centuries. The rediscovery of the old national literature led to a sense of pride and the translation—or adaptation—of original works into English. Ancient sports, dances and entertainments were revived (for instance, the Gaelic Athletic Association created in 1884.) The Gaelic League, founded in 1893 by Douglas Hyde (1860–1949), a Protestant who was to be the first President of the Republic, concerned itself at first with reviving the language but it soon became too immensely popular not to assume a political role and Hyde resigned in 1915 when its initial aim was expanded to the realisation of 'a free, Gaelic-speaking Ireland'.

Such a political goal, too strong for members of the Establishment, was accepted and deemed sufficient by the nationalists in whose ranks were recruited most of those who joined the Sinn Fein ('Ourselves Alone') movement created in 1905, and the Irish Volunteers (1913). The members of The Irish Citizen Army, among the founding fathers of which were James Connolly (1868–1916) and Sean O'Casey, held, however, more mixed opinions. Some members disagreed on the means which should be used to win freedom, influenced as they were by the Fenians of the Irish Republican Brotherhood of James Stephens (1825–1901), who favoured violence to make their country independent. Many had no concern with 'Gaelic' Ireland, wanting only a democratic people's republic in which the working classes, having overthrown the capitalist framework (a much greater source of evil, in their eyes, than British rule), would come into their own at last. The latter conception, shared by O'Casey, had been strengthened by the spectacular development of the Labour movement ever since James Larkin (1876–1947) had started organising Irish workers in 1908 and had launched The Irish Transport and General Workers' Union in 1909; in 1913, although they were ultimately defeated, the workers had managed to paralyse Dublin with a general strike. But it mostly owed its appeal to the appalling conditions of life of the Irish poor in general and the Dublin poor in particular.

The state of things for farmers had certainly improved since the days of the Great Famine of 1845, thanks to the efforts of the Tenant Right League (1850), the Irish National Land League (1879) of Michael Davitt, the Plan of Campaign of 1886, Plunkett's Irish Agricultural Organization Society (1894), and the various legislative measures that such initiatives entailed.

The urban proletariat, on the other hand, could hardly have fared worse. There was, of course, the question of wages and the state of near starvation of large families where the father tended to drown his worries in beer and whiskey as soon as he got enough money for it. But there also was the housing problem in places like the north-eastern parts of Dublin where *The Shadow of the Gunman* is set. In 1913, a

Local Government Board Commission recorded that 21,000 families were living in one-room tenements, of which 9,000 were occupied by four or more persons. In O'Casey's play, Mr Gallagher falls into this category since his tenement houses his two children as well as his wife and himself, his predicament being intensified by other people's children who, on account of the overcrowding of their own lodgings, use his hall as a playground. As for Mr Grigson, he exemplifies, as does Captain Boyle in *Juno and the Paycock*, the selfish tendency of men to resort to drink at whatever cost to their wives and children.

It is through the consciousness of such miserable people (whom O'Casey knew well, having been one of them) that Ireland's conflict is presented by the dramatist, and it is not to be wondered at that they should aspire to a change: they were the first victims of the state of affairs, even though the fight was being fought, in theory, for them.

The conflict began in earnest in 1916, with the coming together of the contradictory forces listed above. Thanks, perhaps, to the onset of the First World War in 1914, in which proletarians were fighting proletarians, Labour partisans and socialists came to think that charity had better begin at home. Nationalists, even when they were originally pacifists, were reminded that England's difficulty was Ireland's opportunity, and the Germans were ready to aid that state of mind. Whatever the reasons, people of varying tendencies joined in the Rising on Easter Monday 1916, and such was their courage and the initial total disbelief of the British that they were able to seize and hold the General Post Office and a few other buildings in Dublin for several days after Patrick Pearse had read a proclamation of an independent Irish Republic—finally to surrender to superior force, including the gunboat used to shell the insurgents' headquarters.

The bulk of the people felt little or no concern, as had been the case with certain previous revolutions (that of 1848, for instance). Dubliners were too poor to be interested in politics, and a number of them participated only by looting the shops—as shown in Act III of *The Plough and the Stars*. Others, whose brothers, fathers, husbands or sons were at that very moment fighting with the British in the trenches (150,000 men in all) could hardly feel sympathetic; this is the reaction of Bessie Burgess in *The Plough and the Stars*:

> there's a storm of anger tossin' in me heart, thinkin' of all th' poor Tommies, an' with them me own son, dhrenched in water an' soaked in blood, gropin' their way to a shattherin' death, in a shower o' shells! Young men with th' sunny lust o' life beamin' in them, layin' down their white bodies, shredded into torn an' bloody pieces, on th' althar that God Himself built for th' sacrifice of heroes! (Act II, p.168)

What changed the face of things was the execution by the British of fourteen of the leaders, including Pearse and Connolly. The country was horrified, and its mood grew more warlike while a cult developed round the new heroes and martyrs. The continuance of martial law and the full powers given to General Maxwell did not help matters, nor the threat of 'conscription' (compulsory enrolment to fight in the First World War), and 'the temper of the city', the words of the politician John Dillon (1851–1927), became 'ferocious'. Meanwhile, Arthur Griffith's (1872–1922) Sinn-Feiners, who had shown a rather tepid enthusiasm for the Rising, were being transformed. They stood for election as Members of Parliament: Count Plunkett, the father of the executed Joseph Plunkett, was returned in January 1917, and De Valera, the future national leader, just out of prison, in July. And those elected refused to take their seats in Westminster, finally forming, in January 1919, a separate Parliament, called Assembly of Ireland, or Dail Eireann, which reissued a Declaration of Independence stating:

> The Irish Republic was proclaimed in Dublin on Easter Monday, 1916, by the Irish Republican Army, acting on behalf of the Irish people. Now, therefore, we, the elected Representatives of the ancient Irish people in National Parliament assembled, do, in the name of the Irish nation, ratify the establishment of the Irish Republic and pledge ourselves and our people to make this declaration effective by every means at our command.

An Irish Government also was formed. The Dail was formally suppressed in September 1919 and in November its headquarters staff was seized together with many important papers. The Assembly, however, continued to meet in secret and the Ministry to do what work it could, in particular in the field of justice, where the British machinery was supplanted by 'Dail courts' to which Irishmen flocked, ignoring the legal institutions of the Crown: by 1921, there were over 900 Parish courts and 70 District courts in operation.

While this was going on, what the Irish called 'the War of Independence' (or 'Anglo-Irish War') and the British merely considered as a wave of criminal acts, was gradually spreading.

In 1919 it essentially took the form of a struggle between the Irish Republican Army reorganised (out of the Volunteers' forces and others) by the revolutionary chief Michael Collins (1890–1922), who added to it a special group of highly trained agents, and the official police, the Royal Irish Constabulary. There were ambushes, attacks against barracks, assassinations by both sides and even an attempt on the Viceroy.

Lloyd George's Government of Ireland Bill was passed in 1920 and instituted two Home Rule parliaments, one in the twenty-six counties of the South and one in the six north-eastern counties, with a *Council of Ireland* to bridge the gap between the two parts of the divided country. This had no effect other than to intensify the conflict. The British therefore used coercion, suppressing organisations, forbidding propaganda, interning suspects, and seeking a means to reinforce the Royal Irish Constabulary. They increased the number of regular troops (the 'Tommies') already stationed in Ireland and recruited two special forces: ex-British privates who found it hard to settle down after the War, and who were paid ten shillings a day for their mercenary services—the so-called 'Black-and-Tans'; and ex-officers, who received a pound a day, and formed an Auxiliary Division of the Royal Irish Constabulary, referred to as 'Auxiliaries' or 'Auxies'.

If the regular troops, the 'Tommies', proved neither better nor worse than occupation troops anywhere, the two special forces were to behave in such a way as to bring horror to everyone, at home and abroad. Protected as they were by the Restoration of Order in Ireland Act of 1920, which gave wide and exceptional power to the military, they raided, looted, arrested, killed, carried out reprisals and, in a few cases, destroyed whole town areas (for example, Cork) or villages (for example, Balbriggan) or fired in cold blood at players and spectators of a Gaelic football match (at Croke Park in Dublin). Neither such exactions, nor summary executions after court-martial, nor the ruthlessness with which a man like the Lord Mayor of Cork, Terence MacSwiney, was allowed to die after a hunger-strike of seventy-four days, did anything, however, to bring the IRA down or the vicious circle of savagery to an immediate end.

Yet the pressure of international and of British liberal opinion, the general weariness and the Irish shortage of money and arms did finally bring about a truce in mid-1921.

As *The Shadow of a Gunman* supposedly takes place in May 1920 and does not include factual elements later than 1921, we might be expected to stop at this point. The composition of the play started, however, in April 1922, the draft of the first act was completed only by October, and the final manuscript handed in at the Abbey on 21 November. We must therefore take a brief look at what was happening then, which explains why the events of earlier years are informed with the atmosphere of disillusionment of the following period. For, in 1920 or 1921, when England and its emissaries were, with some justification, blamed for everything and a common purpose and suffering unified Irishmen, Shields's scepticism and anger would have been out of place. His complaint that instead of the gunmen dying for the people, the people are dying for the gunmen or his conclusion: 'Oh the country is hopeless an' the people is hopeless', which Boyle's 'Th' whole worl's in a state o' chassis' will half-humorously echo, do not belong to the days of the War of Independence but to the time of the Civil War which broke out nearly immediately after.

The truce had been obtained so that negotiations could be opened between Irish leaders and the British Cabinet headed by Lloyd George on a new status for Ireland. The Irish delegates, among whom were Griffith and Collins, did not succeed, in the face of Northern Irish intolerance, in avoiding partition, nor did they win much more for their country than dominion status (the status of Canada, for instance). They signed the treaty reluctantly, to avoid resuming war 'within three days' as Lloyd George had threatened, because, in Griffith's words, the Treaty none the less 'brought back the flag, . . . the evacuation of Ireland after 700 years by British troops, . . . full rights and powers of fiscal control . . . (and) equality with all nations which form the Commonwealth', and, to quote Collins, it gave Ireland a form of freedom, 'not the ultimate freedom that all nations aspire and develop to, but the freedom to achieve it'.

At 2.10 a.m. on 6 December 1921, the Irish 'Free-State' was born. On Wednesday, 28 June 1922, its forces of order had to turn against its Irish opponents, who would be satisfied with nothing short of an independent Republic including all the thirty-two counties, and had seized the Four Courts in Dublin. Ireland 'split from top to bottom' was at war again and though, this time, the enemy was no longer a foreigner, the same tactics were used and the same terror spread. But this time it was reinforced by anger and bitterness over a useless struggle that cost many more lives than the preceding one, as was realised when, in May 1923, De Valera (who had been no innocent in the launching of the conflict) called for a cease-fire.

The Shadow of a Gunman must also be seen against this background of futility and waste.

The Shadow of a Gunman and the theatrical tradition

It was to the famous *Abbey Theatre* in Dublin that Sean O'Casey presented his first plays in circumstances which one of the then directors, Lennox Robinson (1886–1958) later recalled in his *Curtain Up* (1942). He tells how the directors began to receive plays from Sean O' Cathasaigh towards the middle of 1921. These seemed sentimental, and badly constructed. The author divided the world into capitalists and proletarians, the first selfish and licentious, the second pure and noble. Robinson and Lady Gregory read their way through manuscripts, written in a difficult hand with bad ink on poor quality paper. He remarks that they felt inclined to send a rejection slip after reading ten pages or so of each play, but then they would come across flashes of originality that made them read the whole play carefully and then return it to the author with encouraging advice. This advice was not taken, the following plays having the same faults. Eventually, however, they thought one of the plays was hopeful and sent it to Yeats to read. He wrote a vehement criticism of it:

> He saw clearly the merits of the play and saw as clearly its glaring faults. He slashed the author's sentimentality and implored him to write of life as he knew it—it chanced to be the life of the Dublin slums, a subject as yet hardly touched on by our playwrights. The author winced—what author would not?—under this criticism and I have still a letter defending himself, but Yeats's criticism sank in and he writes to me in the October of 1922, 'Many, many thanks for your own kind expression of appreciation, I shall certainly take advantage of your generous invitation to go to see you and talk of my work. I am engaged on a play at present—*On the Run*—the first act is finished and most of the second. It deals with the difficulties of a poet who is in continual conflict with the disturbances of a tenement house, and is built on the frame of Shelley's phrase: 'Ah, me, alas, pain, pain ever, forever'.
>
> A month later the play was finished and delivered. This manuscript was typed 'not faultlessly, I'm afraid, but the result is obviously immeasurably above my fiendish handwriting. I have to thank you and Lady Gregory for the self-sacrifice displayed by the reading of such a manuscript as *The Crimson in the Tricolour*.'
>
> *On the Run* was immediately accepted, I think with no revisions, renamed *The Shadow of a Gunman* and the author Englished his name to Sean O'Casey. His gratitude to Yeats shows itself in the words he wrote in the copy of *Juno and the Paycock* which he gave him: 'The man who by the criticism of a bad play of mine made me write a good one.'*

No wonder then that some historians of literature should have laid stress on O'Casey's debt to the institution which, from the Irish Literary Theatre of 1899, through the Irish National Dramatic Society (St Theresa's Hall, 1902) and the Irish National Theatre Society to the Abbey proper in 1904, had become synonymous with serious Irish drama and attracted the best dramatists: J.M. Synge (1871–1909), W.B. Yeats (1865–1939), Lady Gregory (1852–1932), and George Fitzmaurice (1877–1963), as well as the best actors: the Fay brothers, Arthur Sinclair, Sara Allgood, Maire O'Neill, Barry Fitzgerald, F.J. McCormick and many others.

* Lennox Robinson, *Curtain Up*, Michael Joseph, London, 1942, pp.138–9.

Some critics have even gone so far as to compare O'Casey's and Synge's plays, pointing to the presence of certain common themes, for instance the desecration of the hero (*The Playboy of the Western World*, 1907), the strongly matriarchal nature of the society described (*Riders to the Sea*, 1902), certain similarities in the choice of types (the braggart, for instance) and the serious use of farcical elements, and a similar exploitation of colourful idiomatic speech. Lennox Robinson could thus conclude the passage quoted above:

> I have heard it said—I am sure it was Yeats who told me—that Synge planned to write his next play after *Deirdre of the Sorrows* in the dialect of the Dublin slums. One wonders if his mind from beyond hasn't guided O'Casey. There is in both authors the same intense feeling for characterization, the same bitter humour, the love of fine language, in each dramatist the qualities that lead an audience to love or to hate the author's work.*

Even the significant break with so-called 'peasant drama' which has often been attributed to O'Casey—and it is true that he was the first important playwright in Ireland to shift his scene from country to town, just like James Joyce (1882–1941) in the field of the short story (*Dubliners*, 1914) and in that of the novel (*Ulysses*, 1922)—had been heralded at the Abbey by several dramatists, among whom were Lennox Robinson himself, A.P. Wilson (1880–?; author of *The Slough*, 1914) and Oliver St John Gogarty (1878–1957; author of *Blight*, 1917). Meanwhile, north and south, a realistic trend tended to replace the earlier idealisation in the depiction of Irish life in the work of T.C. Murray (1873–1959), Rutherford Mayne (1878–1967), and St John Ervine (1883–1971) who produced in 1911 a famous play, *Mixed Marriage*, set in Ulster.

It can be said that Sean O'Casey was the Abbey dramatist who accomplished the fusion between the contradictory tendencies of that theatre: tragedy and comedy, realism and poetry. In so doing, and in bringing the people of Dublin to the Irish Dramatic Movement, he probably achieved more for the Abbey than the Abbey had done for him. For too much emphasis should not be laid on its influence on the not-so-young new playwright. From his letters to such critics as David Krause and Harry M. Ritchie, it appears that it was only after the production of *The Shadow of a Gunman* that he saw his first Synge play—which leads Krause to remark that he must have been following his elder instinctively rather than consciously.† As for attending the Abbey, he went there only twice before his first work was staged—he

* Ibid, p.140.

† David Krause, *Sean O'Casey: The Man and His Work*, Macmillan, New York, 1960; Collier Macmillan, London, 1975, p.44.

never had the money to spare—once, in December 1917, to see Gogarty's *Blight*, which was apparently accompanied by Lady Gregory's *The Jackdaw*, and another time, in August 1920, to see George Bernard Shaw's (1856–1950) *Androcles and the Lion* with James Stephens's (1882–1950) *The Wooing of Julia Elizabeth*. It was his first Shaw production, although he had read *John Bull's Other Island*.

The main early influence on O'Casey's drama must therefore be sought elsewhere. He has stated himself that he was no stranger to the European movement and had a knowledge of Strindberg and Ibsen, but that his favourites were the Elizabethans: Shakespeare, of course, but also Webster, Ford, and Massinger, some of the Restoration and eighteenth-century dramatists: Wycherley, Congreve, Goldsmith and Sheridan, the crowd of minor authors represented in Dick's *Standard Plays* (an acting edition with detailed stage directions), and, above all, Dion Boucicault (1820–90), the leading Irish writer of melodramas in the nineteenth century: 'Shakespeare's good in bits; but for colour, and stir, give me Boucicault.'* The claim is perhaps not to be taken over-seriously concerning someone whose aim was box-office success rather than literary quality but Boucicault's influence on acting, on stage direction, on theatrical management and even on playwriting can hardly be overestimated, and in his admiration O'Casey finds himself siding with the most exacting critics. Henry James, in 1975, wrote in *The Nation*:

> Mr Boucicault, both as author and actor, is a great triumph—especially as actor. His skill and shrewdness in knocking together effective situations and spinning lively dialogue are certainly commendable; but his acting is simply exquisite. One is hard cleverness, polished and flexible with use; the other is very like genius.

George Bernard Shaw, in a list of recommended playwrights,† included him in a company with the Greeks, Molière, Goethe and Ibsen. Even J.M. Synge admired Boucicault. Shaw was to pay further tribute to him by imitating the trial scene in *Arrah-na-Pogue* in an equivalent episode of *The Devil's Disciple*, a practice followed by O'Casey, though in a more devious way, in *The Drums of Father Ned* in which he probably created a pastiche of the patriotic melodrama of Boucicault.

Whatever the case, Boucicault was practically O'Casey's first introduction to the theatre, and not altogether a bad one. His playing as understudy, in 1895, for the character of Father Dolan in *The Shaughraun*, has already been mentioned. It was also melodramas by

* *Pictures in the Hallway* (Autobiography, Book 2), Pan Books, L,ondon, 1971, p.26.
† *Collected Letters*, 1874–1897, ed. Dan H. Laurence, New York, 1965, p.570.

Boucicault and others which he saw at the Mechanics, on the very spot which was later to become the Abbey, and to that pre-Abbey stage he certainly owes more than to Yeats's theatre.

He got from such plays a number of things. They include a love of 'tableaux'—hence the pictures in his plays. There is an interest in colour and costume—notice in *The Shadow of a Gunman* Minnie Powell's 'brown tailor-made costume . . . crowned by a silk tam-o'shanter of a rich blue tint' (p.89) and Davoren's defence of her: 'Right glad I am that she thinks of dress, for she thinks of it in the right way, and makes herself a pleasant picture to the eye'. There is a use of various tricks to enforce suspense (omens, for instance, or delays in discoveries) or interrupt awkward developments, or achieve both at once (for instance, Tommy Owens's entrance deferring Minnie's and Davoren's kiss). Music is introduced for atmosphere, song for local colour or character delineation, dance for sensuous joy and total spectacle. There is a juxtaposing of incongruous emotions or remarks (see the end of *The Shadow of a Gunman*) and the alternation of comic and tragic:

> As for blending 'Comedy with Tragedy', it's no new practice—hundreds have done it, including Shakespeare up to Dion Boucicault in, for instance, *Colleen Bawn* and *Conn, the Shaughraun*. And, indeed, life is always doing it . . . There's no tragedy that isn't tinged with humour, no comedy that hasn't its share of tragedy . . . *

Finally, through Boucicault, Sean O'Casey inherited the old stereotype of the 'Stage-Irishman', although he was to alter him in significant ways.

The stage-Irishman was originally made in Britain where, from the Renaissance onward, as servant, soldier or fortune-hunter, he paraded his rags, his bull and blunders, his laughter and tears, his prayers to St Patrick, his brogue and ridiculous name, his glass of whiskey, his amorousness and his shillelagh. But he soon became a character in the hands of Irish playwrights as well, often to the fury of their countrymen, who reacted as early as 1775 when they vented their resentment on Sheridan for his portrayal of Sir Lucius O'Trigger in *The Rivals*. They were slowly reconciled to the type, however, as gradually authors, from John O'Keeffe (1747–1833) to Dion Boucicault, dwelt more and more on the conscious wit and humour of this persona (often brought back from a town to a pastoral setting) and intimated—or even plainly showed—that he was far shrewder than those who sneered at him, and that he could make good use of his uncouth appearance and deceptive innocence. Not so, on the other hand, the serious-

* Quoted in R. Hogan, *The Experiments of Sean O'Casey*, St Martin's Press, New York, 1954, p.177.

minded exponents of the Celtic Revival, though some, like Yeats, discerned some truth in the portrait: 'What they did was not wholly false; they merely magnified an irresponsible type, found oftenest among boatmen, carmen, and gentlemen's servants, into the type of a whole nation, and created the stage-Irishman.'* But Yeats also asserted: 'We will show that Ireland is not the home of buffoonery and of easy sentiment, as it has been represented, but the home of an ancient idealism'.† A few years before, Lady Gregory, in *Collier's Magazine*, 21 October 1911, had stated: 'The Abbey Theatre is a protest against the stage-Irishman, the vulgar and unnatural butt given on the English stage to represent our countrymen. We have destroyed that Scarecrow in the mind.'

Yet, when the riots broke over *The Playboy of the Western World*, some spectators seem to have truly believed that 'the worst specimen of stage-Irishmen of the past is a refined acceptable fellow compared with that imagined by Mr Synge',** and the same thing might have been said of O'Casey's braggarts and paycocks: Seumas Shields, Tommy Owens and Adolphus Grigson in *The Shadow of a Gunman*; Captain Boyle and Joxer Daly in *Juno and the Paycock*; Fluther Good in *The Plough and the Stars*. Some of the devices which O'Casey uses (for example, having the story of how a character behaved under this or that circumstance told twice in a completely different way, like Grigson's attitude in front of the Auxiliary) or even more, some of the linguistic tricks (particularly the repetitions or the misapplied polysyllables) also point directly to the tradition with which we are concerned.

There is an obvious difference, however, which lies less in the method than in the purpose of both Synge and O'Casey. To concentrate on the latter, he uses the stage-Irishman to deflate in an ambiguous way both the type itself—which he exaggerates—and its reverse, the new rollicking hero, whom he shows to be no better. His aim, in other words, is no longer to exploit a set figure; it is a satirical expression of what he believes to be the nation's worst vices.

And the same subtle shift can be said to occur with all the rest of the paraphernalia of melodrama: O'Casey uses the form while changing the intention—which becomes a serious one. The audience is lulled into recognition of familiar types, attitudes, tricks, situations, and then the jarring notes are introduced, the laughter suddenly turns to horror and the expected happy ending to tragedy, even though the last words still belong to the buffoon.

Sean O'Casey never was, as T.R. Henn pronounced him,

* W.B. Yeats, Preface to *Irish Fairy and Folk Tales*, 1892.

† Lady Gregory, *Our Irish Theatre*, Putnam, London, 1913, pp.8–9.

** Quoted in *The Story of the Abbey Theatre*, ed. Sean McCann, Four Square Books, London, 1967, p.134.

'condemned to work without having had any literary training, or aware of any steadying tradition'.* From the very start, O'Casey proved more an innovator than a docile follower in his predecessors' footsteps, more of an experimentalist, like Eugene O'Neill or Brecht, than a traditionalist. He was to remain in movement, blending techniques and changing from a (mostly) naturalist standpoint to expressionism and fantasy with equal literary (though not critical, nor popular) success. Like many great writers he was despised by the intelligentsia for lacking taste, measure, manners and continuity. But his work brims with life, and remains intensely lively on the stage, and this vitality allowed him to influence later creators in his turn: Denis Johnston (*b.*1901), different though he may be; Arnold Wesker (*b.*1932), in spite of the master's dislike for some of his ideas; and Brendan Behan (1923–1964), whose *Hostage* takes up O'Casey's derision of false heroes and visceral hatred of violence and war with some of the same scenic devices and a similar pleasure in songs and words.

O'Casey's drama, rooted in tradition, points to the future.

A note on the text

The Shadow of a Gunman, produced at the Abbey Theatre, Dublin, on 12 April 1923, was first published in *Two Plays: Juno and the Paycock/The Shadow of a Gunman*, Macmillan, London, 1925. An American edition appeared the same year published by Macmillan, New York. An acting edition (with more detailed stage directions) was issued by Samuel Branch, London, in 1926. *The Shadow of a Gunman* was subsequently reprinted in: *Five Irish Plays*, Macmillan, London, 1935; *Collected Plays*, Vol. I, Macmillan, London, 1949; *Selected Plays*, George Braziller, New York, 1954; and in *Three Plays: Juno and the Paycock, The Shadow of a Gunman, The Plough and the Stars*; Macmillan (St Martin's Library), London, 1957. This last edition is the same as that published in paperback by Pan Books, London, 1980, and is the one used in the preparation of these Notes.

* *The Harvest of Tragedy*, Methuen, London, 1956, p.212.

Part 2

Summaries

of THE SHADOW OF A GUNMAN

Detailed summaries

Act I

The first act takes place early one afternoon in a Dublin tenement room, during the Black-and-Tan War. Two men in their early thirties, the pseudo-poet Donal Davoren and his pedlar friend, the cynical Seumas Shields, live here. Davoren's attempts to compose poetry are continually interrupted by the stammering chatter of his would-be religious companion and the numerous invasions of the room by the other residents of the house. The interrupters are, successively, Maguire, another pedlar (or so Shields thinks), who leaves a bag behind before hurrying off on some business to the village of Knocksedan; the Landlord coming for long-overdue rent; Minnie Powell, who is in love with Davoren because, like the other tenants, she believes him to be a gunman 'on the run' (a belief which he foolishly encourages in her); Tommy Owens, a young braggart who interrupts the love scene and finally Mrs Henderson and Mr Gallogher who come to read to Davoren a complaint that they want him to convey to the Republican Court of Justice, leaving him barely enough time on his own with Minnie to kiss her goodbye—she has to get back to work—and type her Christian name and his on a slip of paper.

During the action, a '*Stop-Press*' edition of a newspaper is read out off stage announcing an ambush at Knocksedan where one man, a certain Maguire whom Davoren pretends not to know, has been killed.

The first act ends with Davoren's rhetorical question: 'What danger can there be in being the shadow of a gunman?' which gives the play its title.

NOTES AND GLOSSARY:

Stage directions:

Return Room: a room at the back, at right angles to the line of the street and the rest of the house

tenement house: properly speaking, a house let out in flats; has come to mean a dirty, squalid overcrowded place, a slum

Hilljoy Square: a fictitious name which probably stands for 'Mountjoy Square' in the north-eastern part of Dublin, where O'Casey lived for a while. The place had once been a fashionable residential area, hence its fine Georgian architecture. By 1920, however, only the poorest citizens dwelt there

the Virgin . . . crucifix: most Irish Catholic houses would have a statue of the Virgin Mary and representations of Christ on the Cross or pictures displaying his Sacred Heart. Sometimes, as in *Juno and the Paycock*, a votive light is added

typewriter: the various properties described symbolise the characters. The religious representations underline the protective superstition of Shields. The flowers, the books and the typewriter stand for Davoren's aesthetic aspirations. Typewriters were neither common nor cheap at the time and it may seem rather surprising that the impecunious would-be poet should own one. But the equally impecunious O'Casey had managed to acquire a secondhand typewriter by hire purchase, as he tells us in *Inishfallen, Fare Thee Well*

'the might of design . . . ': Louis Dubedat's creed as expressed in Act IV of George Bernard Shaw's play *The Doctor's Dilemma* (1906)

Text:

at all, at all . . . : Irishisms at the beginning of the play include the repetition of that phrase, others like 'a body' (= 'somebody') , 'says he', 'the like of', 'me boy', 'meself', 'there's the braces after breakin'' ('the braces have just broken') as well as phonetic renderings such as 'callin'' (= 'calling'), 'an'' (= 'and'), 'oul' (= 'old') and so on

bedlam: a lunatic asylum (whose inmates keep shouting and making a noise). A corruption of 'Bethlehem' from the Hospital of St Mary of Bethlehem in London which, from the fourteenth century, specialised in mental cases

Morpheus: Seumas is right: the more famous Morpheus was the son and minister of Somnus, an infernal deity who presided over sleep. At the entrance of their palace were a number of poppies and sleep-inducing herbs

The Angelus: in Roman Catholic countries, the bell rings three times a day (6 a.m., 12 noon and 6 p.m.) for a devotional exercise in honour of the Virgin, beginning *Angelus Domini* ('the angel of the Lord'), commemorating the Incarnation. If 'The Angelus went some time ago' it means here that it is past midday and Seumas is too late to attend church ('get Mass') as it is his duty to do on a Sunday. If he does not go he commits a mortal sin

rounds: Seumas is a pedlar, a travelling vendor of such items as braces and hairpins

a rap: a knock (on the door, for instance)

The land of Saints and Scholars: a medieval hyperbolic description of Ireland common enough to have become a cliché. It is true, however, that the Catholic calendar includes a great many canonised Irishmen and that Irish monks were instrumental in spreading knowledge throughout Europe in the Middle Ages

Kathleen ni Houlihan: an allegorical representation of Ireland as a woman, sometimes young and beautiful, bewailing the loss of her sons and her fields. 'Kathleen ni ('the daughter of') Houlihan' is the subject of many a poem and play (notably, for instance, in the writings of J.C. Mangan and W.B. Yeats)

Shelley's *Prometheus Unbound*: Prometheus was condemned by Zeus or Jupiter, the supreme God of Greco-Latin mythology, to be tied to a rock where a vulture fed upon his liver, which was never diminished, though continually devoured. The English Romantic poet Percy Bysshe Shelley (1792–1822), in his lyrical drama of 1820, tells of Prometheus's courage and his deliverance by Hercules. Davoren's quotation is taken from the beginning of Act I, where it is used as a refrain, as in these lines:

No change, no pause, no hope! Yet I endure.
I ask the Earth, have not the mountains felt?
I ask you Heaven, the all-beholding Sun,
Has it not seen? The Sea, in storm or calm,
Heaven's ever-changing Shadow, spread below,
Have its deaf waves not heard my agony?
Ah me! alas, pain, pain ever, for ever!

Notice the discrepancy between Davoren's woes and Prometheus's!

stained-glass windows: an excellent example of the metonymic figure of style called 'synecdoche' in which though only a part is named ('windows') the whole it belongs to ('church') is understood

jazz dance down below: dancing with pain in hell. Compare further 'suffering the tortures of the damned'

the Black and Tans: (see introduction) unemployed former British soldiers engaged to stop the 'rebellion' in Ireland during the War of Independence of 1919–21. They wore khaki coats with black trousers and black caps and were christened 'the Black and Tans' after a well-known Tipperary pack of fox-hounds

Cuchullian: (more commonly spelt 'Cuchulain') the main hero of the Ulster (or Red Branch) Cycle of medieval Irish epic literature. He was the son of the Celtic god Lug, and his original name was Setanta. But, while still a child, having killed the terrible watch-dog of the Smith Culan, he compensated the owner by taking the animal's place, hence his new name which means 'Culan's hound'. He was renowned for his courage and his strength, which explains Seumas's reference, which must, however, have been considered irreverent by O'Casey's audience as Cuchulain was a favourite with the authors of the Irish Literary Revival and even the military leaders of the 1916 Rising. A bronze effigy (by Oliver Sheppard) actually uses Cuchulain as a symbol of the Irish revolutionary spirit. It is to be found in the Dublin General Post Office, the head-quarters of Pearse and his companions in Easter week

be moonlight: (*Irishism*) by moonlight. The irruption of Maguire and his leaving a bag behind him are a major point in the plot

Knocksedan: a village not far from Dublin

cod: (*slang*) fool

Can't be did: Irish popular use for 'it can't be done'

Irish Republic: Ireland, at that time, was still part of the United Kingdom. Republicans were in favour of total separation

Gael: the Irish are supposed to be, in the majority, of Celtic, Gaelic stock. From the 1890s onwards, an interest in things Gaelic became synonymous with patriotism. This included the original language of the country which had been widely supplanted by English. O'Casey, like Seumas, learnt and taught Gaelic. The repetitions of the statements are not there for the sake of emphasis: Seumas is afflicted with a stammer

Irish Republican Brotherhood: or IRB, the name given in 1873 to the secret society founded by James Stephens in 1858 with the old aim 'to make Ireland an independent democratic republic', by violent means if necessary. This James Stephens (1825–1901) is not to be confused with the poet and novelist of the same name (1882–1950)

rifle levy: money contribution to the fight

the Church refused: members of the IRB and 'Fenians' (thus called after the warriors of Finn in the Ossianic Cycle of the Gaelic saga) were excommunicated by the Roman Catholic hierarchy, at all times conservative and opposed to violence

I tarred a prayer: I wrote a prayer with a tar brush

Pro-Cathedral: the church in Marlborough Street, Dublin, used by the Catholics as (= 'pro') a cathedral, since the oldest ones (Christ Church, and St Patrick's) are used by Anglicans (members of the 'Church of Ireland')

Dark Rosaleen: 'Roisin Dubh' in Gaelic, is another allegorical representation of Ireland. A famous poem by James Clarence Mangan (1803–1849) beginning: 'O my dark Rosaleen,/Do not sigh, do not weep!' bears that title

Balor of the Evil Eye : Balor was chief of the Fomors, the sea-giants of the Gaelic Mythological Cycle. One of his eyes had the power of destroying whatever it looked on

argufyin': arguing, disputing

gostherin': (*Irishism*) behaving in boisterous and swaggering fashion. The word is already to be found in William Carleton's *Fardorougha the Miser* (1839): 'We're idlin' an' gostherin' away our time like I dunna what'. In some English dialects the word appears as 'gauster'

again': against

it ud: it would

billickin': annoying, speaking disobligingly

Be me sowl: phonetic rendering of Dublin pronunciation of 'by my soul'

Them's . . . them notices: a popular English construction in Ireland for 'these are . . . these notices'. Note also: 'It was the ('a') sorry day (when) I ever let you come'

troglodytes: cave-dwellers, cavemen

lodgers: Seumas sublets his room to Davoren who shares it with him

on the run: fleeing, hiding. *On the Run* was the original title of *The Shadow of a Gunman*. 'Sure they *all* think you're on the run' introduces the second major structural element in Act I

raid: the Black and Tans often searched suspect houses. Such a raid is the essential element to the action in Act II

rookery: crowded cluster of tenements

Banba: one of the Queens of the Tuatha de Danaan of Irish Mythology, who represents Ireland

Inisfail: 'the island of Destiny', another of the names for Ireland

Is truagh: a slightly corrupt version of a Gaelic refrain to be found in Thomas Davis's (1814–45) 'Lament for the Milesians', published in *The Spirit of the Nation* (1843). It means 'Would that their descendants but dwelt among us'

Donal Og O'Davoren: most Irish names were anglicised in the eighteenth and nineteenth centuries. With the revival many people reverted to the old form (including O'Casey) or even invented Irish forms for names that were not Gaelic in origin

Fury: furies come to torment Prometheus in Shelley's play

lashins: (*colloquial*) lashings, plenty

Do you be: a common construction in Ireland

stick: (*slang*) bear, put up with

Hooley: a party or dance. Originally a Hindu festivity held at the approach of the vernal equinox, in honour of Krishna and the Gopis or milkmaids, more commonly spelt 'Hoolee' or 'Holi'

I danced rings round me!: I danced a great deal, energetically, skilfully

the two-pair back: the two rooms at the back of the tenement

melodeon: a kind of accordion

Orpheus: in Greek mythology, the son of the Muse Calliope and probably Apollo who gave him a lyre on which he played so marvellously that beasts and nymphs were spellbound

weeshy: (*Anglo-Irish*) tiny
dawny: (*Anglo-Irish*) delicate, insignificant
jars: drinks
the men o' '98: 1798 saw the insurrection of the United Irishmen which was savagely repressed by the British
Arum maculatum, **or Wake Robin:** wild arum
Bobbie Burns: Robert Burns (1759–96), Scottish poet. However, the poem 'Annie Laurie' is not by Burns but by William Douglas (1672–1748)
Robert Emmet: (1778–1803) was executed for trying to seize Dublin Castle, the headquarters and symbol of British rule in Ireland. He was a very popular hero and the subject of many songs, particularly Thomas Moore's 'She is far from the land' which tells of the bereavement of the girl he loved, Sarah Curran
'grasp this sorry scheme ...': From Edward Fitzgerald's (1809–83) translation of *Rubáiyat of Omar Khayyám* (1859):

> Ah Love! could thou and I with Fate conspire
> To grasp this sorry Scheme of Things entire,
> Would not we shatter it to bits—and then
> Re-mould it nearer to the Heart's Desire?
> (LXXIII)

I seen: another instance of the popular Irish confusion between the past participle and the preterite ('I saw')
hard put to it: in difficulties
Ross an' Walpole's: probably a reference to a Dublin shop
There's no flies on ... : (*slang*) he is shrewd, cunning
got me?: understand me?
burgeons: troubles, cares
'Up the Republic': to this day the war-cry of Irish nationalists
'High upon the gallows tree': a famous patriotic song which used to serve as a sort of national anthem before 'A Soldier's Song' was officially adopted by the Irish Republic
Ayryinn: Erin (Ireland)
I.R.A.: the Irish Republican Army, formed by Michael Collins in 1919
Sarsfield ... Vinegar Hill: Tommy Owens is no specialist of Irish history. Patrick Sarsfield was the unhappy hero of the battles of the Boyne (1690), of Aughrim and Limerick (1691), and was killed two years later at

Landen while in the Irish Brigade which was in the service of continental monarchs. His last words are supposed to have been: 'Oh, that this were for Ireland'. The battle of Vinegar Hill is an episode in the 1798 rising. It took place in Wexford on 21 June of that year

belly: not a word to be used in the presence of ladies at the Victorian or Edwardian period

wan ov: One of. Mrs Henderson's speech is transcribed in a phonetic way; her brogue is obviously strong and she uses many Irish phrases and idioms and commits a number of grammatical blunders

more nor: (*Irishism*) more than

the front drawin' room . . . the back drawin' room: the rooms have kept the names they had when only one (rich) family lived in the house. Each room now constitutes a separate lodging

fairity: there is no such word in English, 'fairness' is presumably intended

aforesaid: said before, normally used as a participial adjective in legal documents, but Mrs Henderson is so deep in judicial matters that she overdoes it

cleverality: a pompous word for 'cleverness'

decomposed: a malapropism for 'composed'. A 'malapropism' is a ludicrous misuse of a word, called after the practice of Mrs Malaprop, a character in Richard Brinsley Sheridan's (1751–1816) *The Rivals* (1775). Irish dramatists are very fond of the device.

These presents: (*legal*) 'the present document'

Gentlemen of the Irish Republican Army: from early 1920, the Dail Eireann (the Irish Parliament established by the Sinn Feiners on 21 January 1919) organised its own police and its own law courts in (illegal) opposition to those of the Crown. Irish citizens like Gallogher who had previously resorted to the legal British system now hastened to appeal to the Republican Courts whose business was so pressing (while the royal judges went without customers) that it was very difficult to approach them

That's some swank: (*colloquial*) that's showing them, that's smart

wallop: heavy blow. Note the exaggeration

Deeming . . . : note in Gallogher's letter the mixture of legal jargon, learned polysyllables of Romance origin and faulty popular phrases and syntax

childer: a common form in Ireland for 'children'

unvarnished: a malapropism for 'untarnished'; also a pun with 'furnish' (that is, unvarnished furniture)

Primmy Fashy Case: a vulgar mispronunciation of the Latin phrase prima facie, 'arising at first sight', 'clear at once'

most powerfullest: double superlatives are not unknown in Ireland to enforce a saying, but this one is more powerfully ridiculous than most

writ: wrote. The use is in keeping with the legal atmosphere (a writ is a legal document; to writ, in Anglo-Irish, is to serve a person with a writ or summons)

Sinn Fein Amhain: a tautological use of Gaelic: 'Ourselves (Himself) alone, alone'

pennorth: pennyworth

'clare: declare

mallavogin': (*Irishism*) a piece of my mind, a good reprimand

parrotox: a malapropism for 'paradox', and a pun (on O'Casey's part) with 'parrot', which calls forth Mrs Henderson's winged replies

Stop Press: latest news inserted in a newspaper while it is being printed

a make: (*slang*) a halfpenny

follyin': following

Knocksedan . . . Maguire: an essential point in the plot

County Sligo: it is lucky for the plot that Knocksedan is not situated there, as Maguire would have had some difficulty crossing Ireland from East to West in one afternoon. Sligo is south of Donegal Bay in the north-west

particularated: Gallogher is looking for a learned word meaning 'detailed'. The nearest term would be 'particularised'

mandamus: Gallogher's letter is hardly this: a 'mandamus' is a writ issued by the sovereign or by a court in the king's name

interpretate: the form exists, although it is obsolete, and has the same meaning as 'interpret', but it does not make sense here

supernally: supremely. The word is rare and normally meant 'upwards' or 'celestially'

'Faith of Our Fathers . . .': a well-known hymn by Frederick William Faber (1814–63). Green is the national colour of Ireland

Act II

The second act—it is night now—is far from bringing Davoren any more of the peace and quietness he is seeking. Seumas bothers him, while he tries to write, with a supposed 'tapping' he keeps hearing; with his relationship with Minnie; with the state of Ireland; and with his opinion of the excellence of philosophy over religion, although neither proves to be much help when they hear a volley of shots. Then Mrs Grigson comes in to complain that her husband has not yet returned from the pub, to be followed by the boastful Mr Grigson himself, an Orangeman. A little later it becomes obvious that the house is going to be raided. Davoren feverishly burns the complaint to the IRA and finds that the bag which Maguire had left contains Mills bombs. At this point, Minnie rushes into the room, questions them on their panic, and, out of love for Davoren, takes the bag to her quarters. An Auxiliary enters, threatens the men and searches the place but soon leaves on hearing that there is whisky in the Grigsons' kitchen where Grigson is acting in as cowardly a manner as that of Seumas, the good Catholic.

A commotion and shouts offstage reveal that Minnie has been discovered and, a few minutes later, while Seumas and Grigson are boasting to each other of their cool behaviour (neither has been a witness to the way the other has behaved while the Auxiliaries were searching his room), explosions and rifle-fire indicate that there has been an ambush and we learn of Minnie's death; she has been shot 'while attempting to escape'. A paper was found in her breast with her name and another one, the latter illegible.

Seumas expresses his relief and Davoren, horror-stricken, comes near to realising the perils of his pretence and poetically bemoans the untimely end of his admirer.

NOTES AND GLOSSARY:

The cold chaste moon: the quotation comes from Shelley's *Epipsychidion* ('a soul upon a soul', 1821), II, 281–4. The full stop after 'same' is O'Casey's, as Shelley's line runs on in a half-line, 'And warms not, but illumines'

lilts: (*stage direction*) sings rhythmically

digs: (*colloquial*) lodgings

curfew: as martial law had been proclaimed in Ireland, everybody had to remain indoors at night

the might of design: see note on p.22

tappin': tapping. Seumas thinks the noise is a warning of death

bodes: foretells

there's always something like that heard: death warnings are particularly frequent in Celtic lore. Sometimes an old woman, the Banshee, is heard crying; sometimes the noise is heard of an invisible fairy-carpenter nailing a coffin

fox-trot: a popular ballroom dance at the beginning of the jazz era

Helen . . . Paris: in Greek mythology, Helen, the daughter of Zeus and Leda, and the most beautiful woman of her time, brought about the fall of Troy, where Paris, son of its ruler, had taken her. Her husband, Menelaus, King of Sparta, was supported by other Greeks who besieged Troy for ten years and finally took it by the trick of the wooden horse`

gaddin': rushing

Tricoloured Ribbon: showing the three colours of Ireland, green, white and orange

Tommy: a private in the regular British army

Mons: a town in Belgium, near the French frontier, where the British fought their first battle in 1914

on the run out: notice Davoren's repetition of that cowardly phrase, whereas the other characters use 'on the run' to extol his pretended heroism

barrin': barring, except for

it does be: it is; another instance of the popular use of the auxiliary with 'to be' in Irish-English. Note also the verb in the singular after a plural subject: 'Wasn't there children . . . '

The village cock: Shields's location of the line is exact but Davoren's quotation is not. It should be 'the early village cock', and 'twice'. 'Thrice' is perhaps intended to bring into the quotation a biblical reminiscence, that of St Peter's triple denial of Christ after his Lord's arrest

Bosworth: the scene, near Market Bosworth in Leicestershire, of the last battle of the Wars of the Roses (1485), in which Richard III was defeated and killed

There's plenty of men can't sleep: the omission of the subject relative pronoun (here, 'who') is fairly common in the English spoken in Ireland

beads: a very old Catholic devotion which received its definite Western form in the late fifteenth century through the preaching of the Dominicans is called the Rosary of the Blessed Virgin Mary. It consists of the recitation of a series of one Pater (see further in the same passage 'paternoster', the Lord's Prayer beginning with the words: 'Our Father'), ten Aves ('Hail Mary, full of Grace') and one Gloria ('Glory be to the Father and to the Son and to the Holy Ghost') counting them on a closed string of 165 beads (chaplet). The name was transferred from the prayer to the small globular beads used for the counting or 'telling'

holy water: water blessed by the priest, to be found at the entrance of all Catholic churches and with which the faithful cross themselves. It used also to be sprinkled over the congregation just before Sunday Mass (= Eucharist)

De Profundis: the first Latin words of the psalm recited at burial services: *De profundis clamavi ad te Domine* (Out of the depths have I cried)

creed: or *Credo*, a brief summary of the Christian doctrine which, in its shorter version, begins. 'I believe in God, the Father almighty, maker of heaven and earth'. These words are parodied here

Kathleen ni Houlihan: see note on page 23

'Weep on, weep on . . .': A quotation from Thomas Moore's (1779–1852) *Irish Melodies* (1804–34):

> Weep on, weep on, your hour is past;
> Your dreams of pride are o'er;
> The fatal chain is round you cast,
> And you are men no more

have the wind up: (*slang*) are frightened

Records Office: the building in which official documents are kept

'Death is here . . .': a poem by Shelley published in 1820, the first verse of which is:

> Death is here and death is there,
> Death is busy everywhere,
> All around, within, beneath,
> Above is death and we are death

daily communicant: someone who receives Holy Communion (believed to be the Body of Christ) every day. Seumas is, as we know, no such person as he even misses Sunday mass out of laziness

galvanic battery: a set of primary cells used to galvanise, that is, stimulate, rouse, produce contractions, etc

them windows: Irish popular use for 'these windows'
an' we sittin': while we are sitting, a common Irish use of the absolute participle
'Clare: I declare
he has a sup taken: (*Irishism*) he has drunk too much
turn over a new leaf: mend his ways
Sorra leaf: Devil a leaf!, an Irish expression of doubt
too far gone in the horns: too old
nothin' could fill him with beer: you could never fill him to the top with beer (his power of absorption being what it is)
trilby hat: (*stage direction*) a soft, felt hat with narrow brim and indented crown, called after the heroine of a novel *Trilby* (1894) by George Du Maurier (1834–96)
av: phonetic rendering of Irish pronunciation of 'of'
there's no blottin' it out: there's no denying it
wasn't born in a bottle: the expression means 'wasn't born yesterday' but is used here as a joke on Grigson's drinking
he's fit to take a fall out av Adolphus: have a fight with
informer: someone who betrays his own side or people to the police or the enemy, generally for a reward. In a colonised and divided country like Ireland, informers were particularly numerous, despised and—if caught—punished. See, for instance, the character of Johnny in O'Casey's *Juno and the Paycock*, and see also Liam O'Flaherty's (*b*. 1897) novel *The Informer* (1925) and the recent film, *Ryan's Daughter*
goughers: gougers (swindlers)
deludin': a malapropism for 'alluding'
the Bible: although the bible (or 'Holy Scripture(s)') is the sacred (or 'good') book of all Christians, it more often appears in connection with Protestants than Catholics, as Catholicism paid more attention to sacraments than the Word, and, until recent times, distrusted the personal interpretations that could be made of unannotated versions of the Old or New Testaments. The Bible is therefore mentioned here to indicate Grigson's denomination. Protestants, the majority in Ulster, or Northern Ireland, constitute no more than ten per cent of the population of the present Republic of Ireland, of which they are important and loyal citizens. In 1920 they were divided. If many of them had been or were

'true Irishmen', a large fraction could not accept the end of the union with Great Britain and the overthrow of the King's supremacy. This was particularly true of 'Orangemen' in the strict sense of the word (that is, not merely the heirs of those who fought for William of Orange, a Protestant monarch, against James, who was a Catholic, at the Battle of the Boyne (12 July 1690), but the members of the Protestant Orange Society formed in 1795 'to maintain the laws and peace of the country and the Protestant constitution' and counteract the action of the United Irishmen, who were to lead the 1798 rebellion). It seems that Grigson is an Orangeman in the strict sense of the word since he refers to his 'Chapter' or 'Lodge' ('branch') and sings 'Erin's Orange Lily O', which may be regarded as a sectarian hymn for Northern Irish Protestant extremists. On the other hand, he is obviously muddled, as is shown by his admiration for what he thinks Davoren is; and he will become even more muddled when he realises that the British make no distinction between Irishmen of one creed or another, one of (Protestant) O'Casey's dramatic ironies

have you me?: (*colloquial*) do you understand my meaning?

Tone: Theobald Wolfe Tone (1763–98), one of the founders of the Society of United Irishmen. He secured the help of the French to liberate his country, but they were defeated and Tone was captured, court-martialled and sentenced to be hanged, in spite of his request for a soldier's death by shooting. He then cut his own throat and died of his wounds on 19 November 1798

Emmet: see note on p.27

Parnell: Charles Stewart Parnell (1846–91), nationalist and Home Rule leader, 'Ireland's uncrowned king', whose endeavours came to an untimely end when he was named as co-respondent in a petition for divorce and, the Court having returned a verdict against him, married Mrs O'Shea. If the majority rejected him, a strong minority was, however, to remain fervently faithful to him, as the works of Joyce and Yeats show

no coolness: no unfriendly feeling

Viceroy: the representative of the British Crown in Dublin

Connaught: the western province of Ireland

traneen: the anglicised spelling of Gaelic *traithnín*: a little stalk of grass, (here = a bit)

Ten Commandments: in the Bible, Exodus 20:1–17, the precepts delivered by God to Moses

the Blue Lion: a pub

bag: notice the effect of the discovery on the action of the play

Mills bombs: hand grenades, serrated on the outside to form shrapnel on explosion, invented by Sir William Mills (1856–1932)

pickle: trouble, plight

St Anthony: St Anthony of Padua (1195–1231), a Portuguese Franciscan friar, the object of widespread devotion in Ireland. As he is generally called upon to help to find lost property, his invocation here must be considered as ironical

brunt: the chief stress

Hail, Mary: only a part of the Ave Maria, the angelic salutation to the Virgin, is used by Seumas, interspersed with other exclamations of his own: 'pray for us, sinners, now and at the hour of our death'

act of contrition: a prayer which Roman Catholics say, after confession or at the hour of death, to express regret for their sins and to ask God's forgiveness

if they do aself: (*Irishism*) *even* if they do that *very* thing (that thing *itself*)

''Old the light 'ere': (*stage direction*) Hold the light here. See also ''oo's 'ere' (who's here), 'awd of 'earing' (hard of hearing), ''ow' (how), 'koind blowke' (kind bloke, 'chap'), 'down't (don't), 'han'' (and), 'selt' (celt), 'a lingo (language) of its ahn' (own), 'abaht' (about), all phonetic renderings not, this time, of English spoken in Ireland, but of popular, Cockney (London) English

Auxiliary: (*stage direction*) properly, not a Black and Tan but a member of the so-called Auxiliary Division of the Royal Irish Constabulary, more familiarly known as the 'Auxies'. For the most part, these ex-officers who received a pound a day and had their own dark-blue uniform with Glengarry caps were as bad as, if not worse than, the Black and Tans. They first came to Ireland in Summer 1920

what prawse: what price! would it matter if
grub: (*slang*) food
ikey: smart, shrewd. Derives from Isaac (originally a nickname for a Jew)
kidded: (*slang*) hoaxed, tricked
curer: see following page; Grigson calls whisky his medicine
blaguards: blackguards, scoundrels
Mr Moody, Mr Sankey: Ira David Sankey (1840–1908) was a famous American evangelist who compiled a collection of Gospel Hymns in collaboration with Dwight L. Moody
an he singing': while he was singing
sacret: phonetic rendering of Irish pronunciation of 'secret'. Many nationalist and republican organisations had been (and still were) organised in Ireland as secret societies
Auxsie: Auxiliary
riddled: that is, with bullets
They're after gettin': (*Irish phrase*) they have just got
blew up: blown up
coolin': time to cool her heels; that is, in prison
gosterin': see 'gostherin' on page 25
a stiff upper front: a stiff upper lip (*colloquial*: calm in the face of difficulties)
ambush: in the type of guerrilla warfare of the 1920s in Ireland, the Black and Tans and Auxiliaries constantly came across armed patriots lying in wait for them
off her own bat: (*colloquial*) on her own initiative
buzzom: bosom
Till the silver cord is loosened: the quotation is from the Bible, Ecclesiastes 12:6, which presents a picture of the evil days to come when 'fears shall be in the way', 'or ever the silver cord be loosed, or the golden bowl be broken . . . '

Part 3

Commentary

Reality and imagination in *The Shadow of a Gunman*

Sean O'Casey has often been described—at any rate where the Dublin trilogy is concerned—as 'a realist of the most uncompromising kind' (S. Cowasjee) and even as 'a photographic artist' (A.E. Malone).

External realism

The Shadow of a Gunman sets out to present the atmosphere, the events and the conditions of life among the Dublin poor at a given moment, and it draws on actual happenings and characters. The play succeeds in catching the climate of terror of a city where all the hazards of guerrilla warfare (ambushes, raids, reprisals, manufacturing of bombs, patriots on the run, and so forth) are at work, exactly as *Juno and the Paycock* captures the spirit of insecurity and bitterness of the Civil War. In this respect, O'Casey drew upon an Irish tradition and, by introducing that tradition into drama, whereas it had previously been the province of the novel alone, he became a pioneer. This technique has since been adopted to describe either approximately the same period—for instance, in some of the plays of Denis Johnston or George Shiels (1886–1949)—or the more recent troubles of Northern Ireland, as in *The Freedom of the City* (1974) by Brian Friel (*b.* 1929).

The events which are the result of the situation and conducive to such atmosphere are not only realistic, but they were partly lived by O'Casey himself. If he never stayed in 'Hilljoy Square', there being no such place in Dublin, he did stay in Mountjoy Square—at No.35, where he shared a tenement room with his friend Mícheál Ó Maoláin; and it was during his stay there, on Good Friday, 25 March 1921, that a raid occurred about which both men were to write in their autobiographies and which seems to have closely resembled the one in Act II of *The Shadow of a Gunman*.

In O Maoláin's account in Irish, published in *Feasta* under the title 'Au Ruathar Ud Agus A nDeachaigh Leis', the description given of the room with its two windows, a stretcher bed, and so on, tallies closely with O'Casey's description of the room in the play; if Sean was not actually in possession of a complaint to the IRA, he had the reports of the ICA and was terrifed, as was his friend, by the danger of their being discovered.

In *Inishfallen, Fare Thee Well*, the chapter entitled 'The Raid' presents the author on his own in the room, but several other details correlate closely:

> Sean's eyes were closing, and dimming thoughts swooned faintly from his mind into the humming whine of motor-engines coming quick along the road outside. Up on his elbow he shot as he heard the sound of braking, telling him that the lorries were outside of his house, or of those on either side. Then he shot down again to hide as a blinding beam from a searchlight poured through the window, skimming the cream of the darkness out of the room. It silvered the old walls for a few moments, then withdrew like a receding tide to send its beam on another part of the house. Then there was a volley of battering blows of falling glass that told Sean the panels on each side of it had been shattered by hammer or rifle-butt.
>
> A raid! All the winsome dreams of the house had vanished; sleep had gone; and children dug arms and legs into the tensing bodies of their mothers.
>
> Which were they—the Tommies or the Tans? Tans, though Sean, for the Tommies would not shout so soullessly, nor smash the glass panels so suddenly; they would hammer on the door with a rifle-butt, and wait for it to be opened. No; these were the Tans.*

This passage bears a close resemblance to the stage directions in *The Shadow of a Gunman: 'A volley of shots is heard in a lane that runs parallel with the wall of the back-yard*' (p.111) and '*There is heard at street door a violent and continuous knocking, followed by the crash of glass and the beating of the door with rifle-butts*' (p.121); and to Seumas's remark 'If it's the Tommies it won't be so bad, but if it's the Tans, we're going to have a terrible time' (p.122). This is a distinction which O'Casey took some pain to establish further in 'The Raid', with parts of the dialogue also very similar to that in the play. He tells how the door opened and a torch shone into his eyes. An officer, torch in one hand, revolver in the other, stood inside the door of his room with two soldiers behind him, rifles raised. The officer put his revolver back in its holster and ordered Sean to go out to the street, advising him to put on an overcoat, remarking that it was damned cold outside. Sean considered him a decent man and was thankful the Black and Tans were not there. Then he went out into the hall and bumped into a Tan who was standing there, fingering a heavy revolver. He was asked where he was going:

* Sean O'Casey, *Autobiographies*, Vol.II, Macmillan, London, 1963, p.40.

—Outside to street—officer's orders, said Sean.
—What officer? asked the Tan.
—Military officer, sir.
—Oh! Military officer, eh? Well, we give the orders here—understand?
—Yessir, said Sean promptly.
—Are you a Sinn Feiner? he questioned, twisting the gun in his hand.
—A Sinn Feiner? Me? No fear.
—You were one, then.
—No; never, said Sean emphatically. Thank God, thought Sean, he didn't ask if I had ever been a Republican. The ignorant English bastard doesn't know the difference.
—Well, you're an Irishman, anyway—you can't deny that!
—No, sir, I can't deny that: I'm an Irishman, right enough.
—Well, shout To Hell with Ireland, and you can go—no mutter, but a shout the house can hear. Now!
But Sean fell silent. God damn him if he'd do that! He knew his face was white; he felt his legs tremble; but he fell silent, with a stubborn look on his face.
—Go on, you Sinn Fein rat, shout it!
A streak of light fell on them, and Sean saw the young officer coming to them. He stopped, looked at Sean, then looked at the Tan.
—What's wrong here? he asked. Let that man go into the street.
—You mind your own damned business, snarled the Tan.
—I am minding it, said the young officer. I happen to be an Irishman, too. Have you any objection to it?
—I don't take orders from you! said the Tan roughly.
—I'm not sorry for that, the officer said; but this man does—didn't I give you an order to go into the street? he asked, turning to Sean.
—Yessir.
—Carry it out, then, he said sharply; and Sean, turning swiftly, made a quick march through the hall, out by the door, into the street.*

Other parallels with *The Shadow of a Guman* are just as interesting: the visit of a neighbouring woman while Sean was lying in wait in his bed, which recalls the stream of visitors to Davoren's and Seumas's room, or his thoughts of romantic poetry, although it was the American poet Walt Whitman rather than Shelley that came to his mind:

* Autobiographies, Vol.II, pp.49–50.

Azrael, Azrael, gentle, dignified being of spirit, graceful spirit of death, come, and minister unto us, and save us merry gentlemen!

Come lovely and soothing death,
Undulate round the world, serenely arriving,
Arriving
In the day, in the night, to all, to each,
Sooner or later, delicate death.

Ah! Whitman, Walt Whitman, you never knew the Tans! Death doesn't arrive serenely here, his hands are desperate, and neither is he delicately formed. Here the angel of death is a biting bitch!*

The autobiographical story also explains Shields's mention that

There's a stable at the back of the house with an entrance from the yard; it's used as a carpenter's shop. Didn't you often hear the peculiar noises at night? . . . I wouldn't be surprised if they were manufacturin' bombs there, (p.112)

It also offers the circumstantial details of Minnie's arrest and her final gesture of patriotic defiance:

He saw a commotion round the door of the house he lived in. He mooched over till he was beside the steps to look over the shoulders of a rank of soldiers. A prisoner! Who could it be? He whisperingly asked the soldier in front of him what had happened.

—An awrsenal! whispered the soldier hoarsely. Rear of th' 'ouse, an awrsenal discovered! 'Nough gelignite to blow up 'ole neighbourhood. A blighter there drew a gun, but was shot through hand afore 'ee could pull trigger. 'Ere's the bawstard coming.

Amid a group of soldiers with rifles at the ready marched a thin forlorn figure, but the lips in the pale face were tight together, and the small head was held high. Peering closer, Sean saw that handcuffs kept the two small hands locked together, and that from one of them red blobs were dripping on to the white frost on the path, leaving little spots behind like crimson berries that had fallen on to snow. In the hall he heard the voice of Nellie shouting.

—That's me husband! he heard her shout; a good man an' a brave one! Yous'll never shoot the life outa Ireland, yous gang o' armed ruffians! Here, take me, too, if yous aren't afraid. Keep your pecker up, Charlie—Ireland's with you!

Sean peered closer. Good God—the prisoner was the timid, insignificant Charlie Ballynoy who took no interest in politics! A lorry, full of soldiers, swirled into the kerb. The handcuffed prisoner was

* *Ibid., pp.42–3.*

> pushed and lifted into it. Standing there in the middle of the soldiers, with the searchlight covering him with glory, he help up his iron-locked hands from which clouts of blood still dripped.
>
> —Up th' Republic! he shouted with the full force of his voice.*

No wonder *The Shadow of a Gunman* appeared so realistic. Indeed, as Lennox Robinson was later to recall:

> We thought it was necessary to print a note on the programme assuring the audience that the lorry sounds and the rattle of machine-guns were only stage-effects. If we had not done this the audience might have fled in terror from the theatre . . . [O'Casey] disturbed me by saying at rehearsal that all the characters were taken literally from life, that so-and-so was Jackie—and another character Jim—Would they, I wondered, come to the back-pit, recognize themselves and wreck the theatre? He reassured me. They never visited a theatre, he named the pubs in which they would inevitably be found.‡

This is a statement that later critics have been apt, rightly or wrongly, to take literally, and more so than the *Autobiographies* would endorse. Thus Saros Cowasjee writes:

> Seumas Shields, the cowardly and voluble pedlar, is a caricature of O Maoláin. Minnie Powell, the brave girl for whom love is greater than the Republic, has her realistic basis in many young women in Ireland who fought for Ireland's freedom; perhaps in Linda Kearns who was sentenced to ten years' imprisonment for carrying ammunition. Maguire, the man of much action but few words, is possibly modelled on a Seumas McGowin who once belonged to the Citizen Army; and Adolphus Grigson, the first of O'Casey's brilliant braggarts, was in real life a printer's compositor.**

Internal realism

Sean O'Casey is concerned with outside reality and can be said to have an Ibsenite obsession with man's plight in society; yet he appears still more interested in man at war with his own nature, an inside realism, in the Strindberg tradition. In this aspect of his plays, there are again strong autobiographical links. In 'Hail and Farewell', the chapter which precedes 'The Raid' in *Inishfallen, Fare Thee Well*, O'Casey tells of his inability to write while living with his brother:

* *Autobiographies*, Vol.II, p.50.

‡ Lennox Robinson, *Curtain Up*, Michael Joseph, London, 1942, pp.139–40.

** *O'Casey*, Oliver & Boyd, Edinburgh & London, 1960, pp. 19–20.

> Sean was trying to think out the words of a song in dead of night when he heard the heavy, lurching steps stumbling up the stairs and the raucous, beery voice forcing itself to shape a song, masquerading a spurious delight in the heart of the braggart, hating himself. From the corner of an eye he saw the tousled figure staggering into the room, knocking clumsily and intentionally against the table at which Sean was sitting, while an envious, dirty hand, sliding along it, sent the little ink-bottle flying to the floor. Sean said nothing, but sat quietly where he was.
>
> —Writin', be God, again! murmured the blurred voice of his brother; some fellas are able to give themselves airs! Scholar, is it? Scholar, me arse! Well, th' ink's gone, so wha'll we do now? Here's one who's forgotten moren' some'll ever learn. There's a man here. Takes a few dhrinks, but a man, all th' same; a man with two good mitts. Writin'! If I was someone, I'd thry to be a man first! But Sean sat still, quiet, where he was.*

O'Casey was thus obliged to move, just as Davoren contemplates doing. In spite of this, and the second-hand typewriter they both managed to get, the resemblances are rather moral and aesthetic, however: both men are representative of the poetic tendency with its corollary of inactivity and cowardice in the face of physical danger; both are authors who, at the beginning, tended towards a kind of escapist writing (O'Casey's poetry resembled Davoren's).

Davoren is not, however, the only character in conveying O'Casey's states of mind. Seumas Shields also represents a stage of his evolution and a side of his personality: the cynical, disillusioned soldier of the Irish Citizen Army who failed to play any significant part in the Rising and tends to believe in the gun as long as there are no guns to be found in the country. There is no doubt that Shields's remembrances of things past are also O'Casey's:

> I don't want to boast about myself—I don't want to boast about myself, and I suppose I could call meself as good a Gael as some of those that are knocking about now—knocking about now—as good a Gael as some that are knocking about now,—but I remember the time when I taught Irish six nights a week, when in the Irish Republican Brotherhood I paid me rifle levy like a man, an' when the Church refused to have anything to do with James Stephens, I tarred a prayer for the repose of his soul on the steps of the Pro-Cathedral. (p.84)

And the same can be said of the character's evolution towards an unpatriotic pacificism:

* *Autobiographies*, Vol.II, p.31.

> The country is gone mad. Instead of counting their beads, now they're countin' bullets; their Hail Marys and paternosters are burstin' bombs—burstin' bombs, an' the rattle of machine-guns; petrol is their holy water; their Mass in a burnin' building'; their De Profundis is 'The Soldiers' Song', an' their creed is, I believe in the gun almighty, maker of heaven an' earth—an' it's all for 'the glory o' God an' the honour o' Ireland'.
>
> (p.110)

O'Casey's aim, however, in telling of such moods and changes is not prompted by any need for a true confession, a realistic presentation of himself, but by a desire to study the motives and the shortcomings of men in general.

Conclusion

Despite the realism of *The Shadow of a Gunman*, there is of course a considerable gap between its effect and that of so-called 'photographic art'; even the parallel with the *Autobiographies* is not total, and then the *Autobiographies* themselves are works of re-creation, arranged versions—though perhaps to a lesser extent than in the play—of basic events which we shall never encounter in their reality.

Like any author, O'Casey drew on personal experiences, but the additions to and subtractions from such experiences are such as to be beyond the scope of any 'photographer', not to mention the concentration of events in time, space and setting and the limitation of the number of characters: for example, the increase in suspense brought about by the bag of bombs; the intensification of emotion caused by the melodramatic death of an innocent young woman; the focusing of small talk or random phrases on main issues such as nationalism, politics, poverty and the fear of being moneyless (Mrs Grigson wondering 'Do the insurance companies pay if a man is shot after curfew?'—even though she is sincerely concerned with the welfare of her good-for-nothing husband whose death would not leave her any the worse); the depth added by the religious and historical dimension; the stylisation.

If this is realistic writing it is realism thoroughly modified. But the aim of the author is only partly the depiction of reality: the main theme of *The Shadow of a Gunman* is not, perhaps, Dublin tenement life in the Black and Tan war but rather an imaginative study in human illusion, an account of how far human beings can retreat from actuality to fantasy and of the comic and tragic results of such an attitude.

All characters in the play resort to dream and picture themselves (and often other people) differently from what they are; in this respect it is not only Davoren who is a 'shadow'—and some are brought back to earth for, to answer the poet's question, there is indeed danger in being a shadow. All possible forms of escapism are touched upon and all pretences revealed for what they are: the would-be hero is shown to be a poltroon where the 'ordinary' girl proves a heroine, although for the wrong motive; patriotism is repudiated for its sighing and weeping and its cult of the past; poetry is shown to be inadequate, as well as philosophy or religion, both 'forgotten in the violent fear of a nervous equality' (p.111).

The play is, in fact, animated by a double movement: from reality to imagination, from imagination to reality. In the light of O'Casey's further development, Denis Johnston was to remark:

> It is becoming more and more clear that as a realist he is an impostor. He will tell you the name and address of the person who made each individual speech in any of his plays, but we are not deceived by his protestations. His dialogue is becoming a series of word-poems in dialect; his plots are disappearing and giving place to a form of undisguised expressionism under the stress of a genius that is much too insistent and far too pregnant with meaning to be bound by the four dismal walls of orthodox realism.*

The Shadow of a Gunman already presents the future O'Casey in the making.

Comedy or tragedy? O'Casey's 'message' in *The Shadow of a Gunman*

Apart from the question of determining whether or not *the Shadow of a Gunman* is a realistic play, a bone of contention divides O'Casey's critics as to whether his play is comic or tragic; and whether it aims at transmitting a message, and, if so, what sort of message.

The Shadow of a Gunman as comedy

The very nature of O'Casey's inquiry into the motivations and mechanisms of men and women—where self-exposure takes place rather than self-discovery and change—invites comic treatment. The same might be said also of the setting, which is one of everyday life, even though the circumstances are exceptional.

Both the method O'Casey employs and the elements he selects are indeed mostly comic, to the very end of the play. He deliberately avoids concluding with Davoren's poetic self-accusation: 'Oh, Donal

* 'Sean O'Casey: an appreciation', in *Sean O'Casey* (Modern Judgements Series), ed. Ronald Ayling, Macmillan, London, 1969, p.85.

Davoren, shame is your portion now till the silver cord is loosened and the golden bowl be broken. Oh, Davoren, Donal Davoren, poet and poltroon, poltroon and poet!', preferring Seumas's clownish *idée fixe*: 'I knew something ud come of the tappin' on the wall!'

There is, to start with, the pervading comedy of character with, undoubtedly, Seumas Shields as a main beneficiary; in fact he would be quite odious otherwise, and is thus kept from giving that impression —at any rate until the penultimate moment when he proves unable to show the least concern for anyone except himself or the least pity for the dead girl, Minnie, to whom he owes his life. Seumas's personality has numerous elements of a traditional comic character: he is lazy, slovenly, procrastinating, miserly, superstitious and cowardly; he has blinded himself to his own defects and only sees them in others, absurdly denouncing them instead. This is to be found, for instance, when, at the beginning of Act I, he complains of Maguire not turning up: 'Have everything packed and ready!' he says repeatedly while he is hardly out of bed. 'And have you everything packed and ready?', Davoren ironically asks, to be answered: 'What's the use of having anything packed and ready when he didn't come?' (p.81). Much the same attitude, and the same mode of presentation, are seen when Seumas's personal hygiene is disclosed:

SEUMAS: I don't think I need to wash meself this morning; do I look all right?
DAVOREN: Oh, you're all right; it's too late now to start washing yourself. Didn't you wash yourself yesterday morning? . . .
SEUMAS: That fellow Maguire . . . he's almost too lazy to wash himself.

(pp.82–3)

And, though he complains of other people's lack of honesty, if he counts his spoons when he has discovered that some of the parcels contained eleven and not the expected twelve, it is in no altruistic mood: 'I'd never be easy in me mind thinkin' there'd be more than a dozen in some o' them' (p.83).

Next to the pedlar the most memorable comic characters in the play are undoubtedly the two 'paycocks', Tommy Owens and Adolphus Grigson, and Mrs Henderson, with her habit of using words she does not understand and her trick of parading Mr Gallogher as some animal in a circus.

The other women are not without their amusing or ridiculous foibles. Mrs Grigson does not know how to make a choice in the details of her lengthy speeches: 'Adolphus, Mr Shields, after takin' his tea at six o'clock—no, I'm tellin a lie—it was before six, for I remember the Angelus was ringin' out an' we sittin at the table . . .' (p.113). She simply cannot stop talking at all, and is therefore partly responsible for Adolphus's ill treatment of her, all the more so as—after criticising him—she pathetically (and ludicrously) cringes before him:

> MRS GRIGSON: . . . if I was a young girl again I'd think twice before gettin' married . . . Is that you, Dolphie, dear? . . . Dolphie, dear, mind yourself . . .
>
> ADOLPHUS GRIGSON: I'm all right; do you see anything wrong with me? [he is drunk]
>
> MRS GRIGSON: Of course you're all right, dear; there's no one mindin' you. (pp.114–15)

Her use and abuse of terms of endearment do her little credit, either in her relationship with her husband, or in the eyes of the audience.

Minnie Powell is shown to be excessively naïve and incapable of concentration. The stage directions state: '*like all of her class, Minnie is not able to converse very long on the one subject, and her thoughts spring from one thing to another*' (p.90). A moment before, her ignorance had been the source of a comic moment:

> MINNIE: You know Tommy Owens, don't you? . . . he's a gorgeous melodeon player!
>
> DAVOREN: A gifted son of Orpheus, eh?
>
> MINNIE: (*who never heard of Orpheus*) You've said it, Mr Davoren: the son of poor oul' Battie Owens . . . (p.89)

Davoren, also enters the realm of comedy on occasions, through the exaggeration and ill-timing of his poetic flights and during his bout of boasting to Minnie who thinks him a gunman on the run:

> MINNIE: Do you never be afraid? . . .
>
> DAVOREN (*delighted at Minnie's obvious admiration; leaning back in his chair, and lighting a cigarette with placid affectation)*: I'll admit one does be a little nervous at first, but a fellow gets used to it after a bit, till, at last, a gunman throws a bomb as carelessly as a schoolboy throws a snow ball. (p.92)

Of course, Davoren has never seen a bomb in his life; he will, and his 'carelessness' will not be very obvious, particularly to Minnie (compare '*Davoren reclines almost fainting on the bed . . . Minnie alone retains her presence of mind*', pp.121–2). In another scene, Davoren's cowardice in real life is again in contrast to his fanciful courage and the comfort he derives from philosophy: 'Philosophy is mine; philosophy that makes the coward brave; the sufferer defiant; the weak strong; the . . (*A volley of shots is heard . . . philosophy [is] forgotten . . .*)' (p.111).

In one production of *The Shadow of a Gunman* Davoren actually flung himself under the bed at this point—an instance of the comedy of situation which recurs frequently throughout the play, sometimes touching on the farcical (think, for instance, of the breaking of Seumas's braces just after they have been described as worthy of the Irish Hercules, Cuchulain). Several traditional comic techniques are also employed: stammering (Seumas); drunkenness (Owens, Grigson); typical comic encounters such as that between tenant and landlord, or bully and victim. The encounter between the Auxiliary and Davoren provides a good example of the latter:

> THE AUXILIARY: 'Ow is it you're not in bed?
>
> DAVOREN: I was in bed; when I heard the knockin' I got up to open the door.
>
> THE AUXILIARY: *You're* a koind blowke, you are. Delighted, like, to have a visit from us, ay? Ah? (*Threatening to strike him*) Why down't you answer?
>
> DAVOREN: Yes, sir.
>
> (pp.122–3)

There are also the comic interruptions (Minnie's and Davoren's love scene and kiss), and the comic reversals, the best of which is the bully Grigson being bullied in his turn, made to sit up in bed, his hands crossed on his breast, his eyes looking up at the ceiling, singing a hymn.

The comedy of words is even more pervasive, however, than the comedy of situation. The characters' accents are funny, whether Irish or Cockney, and so is often their use of dialectal phrases, words and forms. Malapropisms and deformations of words or names abound, particularly with Mrs Henderson, who transforms paradox into 'parrotox', speaks of a letter 'decomposed by a scholar' and describes Gallogher ('Gallicker') as a man of 'unvarnished' respectability. History also is deformed by Tommy Owens's splendid anachronism as he claims to quote the words of Patrick Sarsfield (who died in 1693) at the Battle of Vinegar Hill which took place in 1798.

Verbal exaggeration and ludicrous images flourish throughout the play. Mr Gallogher's letter to the IRA is 'the most powerfullest' letter Tommy has ever heard read (p.101); and the singing of his children—so says Mrs Henderson—would 'make your heart thrill like an alarm clock' (p.103); Seumas takes less notice of his neighbours trying to wake him up than Davoren would of 'the strumming of a grasshopper'; Mrs Grigson, frightened by the arrival of the Auxiliaries, remarks: 'There's not a bit of me that's not shakin' like a jelly' (p.126).

The discrepancy between reality and the way it is verbally described is a fertile source of comedy. One particularly successful example is Seumas's and Grigson's retelling of their interview by the Auxiliary. Seumas, who, when asked what his name was, was not even courageous enough to give it in the Irish form and had stammered his fear of the gun, describes himself as perfectly cool; and Grigson, who lay whining on his bed, boasts of having 'kept a stiff upper front' (p.129). Among this battery of comic devices, we also find the highly effective use of sarcasm:

DAVOREN: How is it you never said anything about this [the manufacturing of bombs nearby] before?
SEUMAS: Well—well, I didn't want—I didn't want to—to . . .
DAVOREN: You didn't want to what?
SEUMAS: I didn't want to frighten you.
DAVOREN: (*sarcastically*): You're bloody kind! (pp.112–13)

(the last words anticipating those of the Auxiliary). We also find genuine wit and humour, especially in the two protagonists' remarks:

DAVOREN: A man should always be drunk . . . when he talks politics—it's the only way in which to make them important. (p.90)

SEUMAS: . . . there's always something like that [a tapping] heard when one of our family dies.
DAVOREN: . . . there's a hell of a lot of things heard when one of your family lives. (p.107)

SEUMAS: Wasn't there children in the last place you were in too?
DAVOREN: Ay, ten; and they were all over forty. (p.109)

SEUMAS: [The Tommies] don't give a God's curse who they plug.
DAVOREN: Maybe they ought to get down off the lorry and run to the Records Office to find out a man's pedigree before they plug him. (p.110)

GRIGSON (*drunk*): . . . Adolphus Grigson wasn't born in a bottle.
DAVOREN: A most appropriate place for him to be born in. (pp.115–16)

Although O'Casey is no adept of the witty Comedy of Manners in which the Irish have excelled, from Farquhar and Congreve, Sheridan and Goldsmith to Oscar Wilde, it is obvious that he can master some of its components. No wonder that critics such as Kenneth Tynan have thought that 'the element of volatile caricature . . . is the glory of the play, its essence and its life', adding: 'O'Casey belongs to the boisterous gallery of Irish satirists, comedians, ironists and mock-heroic wits . . . He means us to laugh at the plight of two men trapped in a lie, and he expects of his small-part players the pace and timing of vaudeville.'*

* Quoted by David Krause, 'Sean O'Casey', in Richard J. Finneran (ed.), *Anglo-Irish Literature: A Review of Research*, MLA, New York, 1976, p.493.

The Shadow of a Gunman as tragedy

It could be argued that O'Casey's boisterous and abundant vitality is more at ease with comedy than tragedy and that he has a surer gift in delineating the comic characters: Seumas is definitely livelier and more colourful than Davoren, Mrs Grigson than Minnie. Some critics, however, have complained that in productions of *The Shadow of a Gunman* too much stress has been placed on the comedy, especially on the scene-stealing role of Seumas Shields, with the result that the tragic tone and theme have been wrongly minimised.

For there are indeed tragic elements, albeit sometimes discreet. Consider, for example, Seumas's remark: 'it's safer to have a woman in the room' (p.125); male selfishness reaches the level of tragedy here. Some tragic instances are, however, unmistakable: the plight of the poor people in general, the artist's incapacity to accept and be accepted by his social milieu, the narrow margin between love and death, Minnie's untimely end. If, in all this, it is melodrama rather than tragedy that comes to some critics' minds, this is none the less tragic, not comic, melodrama.

If tragic elements of the play are greatly outnumbered by the comic ones, this is no reason to doubt its tragic quality; for this tragic quality resides not in the balance of elements, but in the author's purpose, which is anything but amusing. Comedy turns into tragedy, while also serving to hide it—a cathartic function that shields both the author and his characters from their utter despair in the face of their impotence, their leaders' incompetence, their country's state of chaos and the general egotism and imbecility of the victims. Ronald Ayling has put it well:

> For O'Casey the grotesque was a means of expressing tragedy and horror on a large scale, without toppling the drama into complete bathos . . . The plays are conceived as social or national tragedies in the widest possible sense, realising the fearful situation of a whole class, an entire society as much as of individuals like Minnie Powell, Juno Boyle, or Nora Clitheroe. Even as early as *The Shadow of a Gunman* the largely farcical realisation of Shields's cowardice is the fore-stage accompaniment to Minnie Powell's arrest and death (which take place off-stage) . . . The comic elements are not there for light relief, though they naturally perform that function. However enjoyable or hilarious the alcoholic fantasies and mock heroic gestures may be, the moral irresponsibility of the menfolk in each of [the] early plays is equal in tragic depth to the formal expression of a nation's grief represented in the sufferings of the womenfolk.*

* *Sean O'Casey* (Modern Judgements Series), Macmillan, London, 1969, p.23.

Sean O'Casey's message in the play

One cannot discuss the 'seriousness' of a play simply in terms of the comparative weight of its comic or tragic elements, for seriousness is in no way linked to genre: there can be a deadly serious side to comedy. But this question apart, there are some critics who deny that there is any serious import behind Sean O'Casey's work, and who consider that he has no clear ideas to put forth. Some of these critics find O'Casey's ideological framework unconvincing; others find that the emotional content obscures any clear thinking and weakens any political or moral conviction which the work is supposed to bear.

O'Casey is, however, neither a disciple of the theatre of ideas nor a propagandist and partisan pamphleteer. His thought, rather, amalgamates several systems and creeds, including socialism (and even communism to which he remained faithful in his own way), and the New Testament, fused into one on several occasions (for instance when he wrote in *The Irish Statesman*, 7 February 1925, 'My sympathies were always with the rags and tatters that sheltered the tenement-living temples of the Holy Ghost'). Such statements demonstrate that his tendencies are by no means concealed, but as a good dramatist he avoids black and white portraits—even of the people he loves.

O'Casey may appear limited: but his is a philosophy of life rather than an intellectual system, as he himself said to Don Ross in 1958:

> ROSS: Do you think that this play of yours, *The Shadow of a Gunman*, has got anything to say to us today about politics? Is there a contemporary meaning?
>
> O'CASEY: Well, so they tell me . . . they tell me that it's philosophy rather than politics. I don't think there are any politics in the play—that is current politics. But it's philosophy, it's general philosophy.
>
> ROSS: What's the philosophy of the play?
>
> O'CASEY: Well, I think the general philosophy of the play is the bewilderment and horror at one section of the community trying to murder and kill the other. Against war, against strife. My philosophy is—speaking directly now—that life, life ought to be a safe thing to live. It oughtn't to be dangerous to live life, ought it? I think that all our efforts should be concerned with making life safe, not making it dangerous. That's why I'm against the hydrogen and all these atomic bombs and against war. I think they're making life dangerous instead of making life safe. That's my philosophy, and I think that's the philosophy that's in *The Shadow of a Gunman*.*

* *The Sting and the Twinkle*, ed. E.H. Mikhail and J. O'Riordan, Macmillan, London, 1974, p.91.

Neither a political thinker in spite of his devotion to Marxism, nor a mystic in spite of the part played by religion in his plays, O'Casey appears as a humanist, more interested in people than in ideas, or even technique. 'I spoke to him of technique', J.L. Hodson writes: '"I abominate it" he said. "They tell me *The Shadow of a Gunman* breaks all the rules. If the characters live and the play holds the audience, that's enough!"'*

The Shadow of a Gunman as drama and literature

'They tell me *The Shadow of a Gunman* breaks all the rules.' O'Casey's remark refers to the fairly large body of hostile criticism which greeted his first performed play, too significant to be simply dismissed, and some of it not altogether misjudged as assessments of the work of a beginner.

A beginner's faults

It is difficult not to agree with those who consider that there might valuably be fewer characters in the play, and that their roles might be less episodical. Too many characters result in a lack of delineation, and if such a shortcoming in no way tarnishes the presentation of Davoren, Seumas or Minnie, minor figures tend to appear as illustrations, voices, puppets, or as mere caricatures. Then, Tommy Owens, Mr Mulligan (the landlord), Mrs Henderson and Mr Gallogher would not have been dropped at the end of the first act to be replaced by Mr and Mrs Grigson, whose introduction would have been better at an earlier stage.

It is also difficult not to agree that *The Shadow of a Gunman* bears traces of having been conceived as a one-act play—the only form O'Casey was familiar with when he wrote it—and artificially expanded into two acts with a repetitive pattern and a juxtaposition of episodes. To take up some further points: leaving a suitcase with unknown contents in Seumas's room is perhaps clumsy as a device and the suspense may be broken for some readers and spectators by learning too soon that its owner, Maguire, is a gunman; more embarrassing is what Frank O'Connor, in *The Backward Look*, called 'the neatest trick in theatrical history' and 'a shocking bit of construction', namely that 'Maguire appears, leaves for a place called Knocksedan, thirty miles away, joins some other Republicans there in an attack on a British column, is killed, identified and reported dead in a Stop Press edition which is on sale in the Dublin streets ten minutes after his departure'.†

* *The Observer*, 22 November 1925; quoted in *The Sting and the Twinkle*, p.22.
† Frank O'Connor, *The Backward Look*, Macmillan, London, 1967, pp.217–18.

If the climax of the play is considered to occur when Davoren and Seumas cowardly allow Minnie to take the bag of bombs to her room, then it comes too early, as Robert Hogan remarks, 'and is weakened by the number of exciting offstage events which are needed for the dénouement but which only the minor characters participate in. When it is necessary for minor characters to carry the burden of the play in crucial moments offstage, a diminishing of effect and a blurring of outline seem inevitable.'*

Finally, in respect of the language and style of *The Shadow of a Gunman*—particularly if compared to the later plays—the reader may get a feeling that these are slightly out of focus, which would perhaps explain why derogatory and yet contradictory judgements have been passed by critics, some finding O'Casey's idiom too realistic and asserting that the speech of townsmen, as transcribed by the playwright, 'can rarely carry any literary weight'† ; others discerning 'a dangerous tendency' on the part of the author 'to manufacture a sort of slum Kiltartan' (the allusion is, of course, to the literary type of peasants' Anglo-Irish made popular by Lady Gregory). The latter remark is by the Irish critic P.S. O'Hegarty. It was taken up some thirty years later by Jacques Barzun who says of O'Casey's 'ornate prose':

> it is what many people think the Irish speak to one another all day long. This is observably not so. The prose, which is as artificial as that of *Finnegans Wake*, was invented by J.M. Synge . . . to suggest what his peasants dimly felt in their bosoms, not what they could improvise when you asked them for a night's lodging. O'Casey adapted the technique to his Dubliners' more sordid communications.**

There is also the rather immature habit, not only of Davoren, but also of Seumas—or rather of self-taught Sean O'Casey himself—of revelling in quotations and allusions to show off their knowledge, and of all speakers to become, perhaps, unduly fond of words, particularly adjectives.

A playwright's conscious choice

Most of the criticism cited above seems well-founded—but not all of it. The theatrical and imaginative nature of *The Shadow of a Gunman* is

* Robert Hogan, *The Experiments of Sean O'Casey*, St Martin's Press, New York, 1960, p.34.

† Raymond Williams, *Drama from Ibsen to Brecht*, Penguin Books, Harmondsworth, 1973.

** In *Sean O'Casey* (Modern Judgements Series), ed. Ronald Ayling, Macmillan, London, 1969, p.124.

not taken sufficiently into account by those who see a weakness in the time-scale of events in the plot: the time of the clock and dramatic duration do not necessarily coincide. Nor does O'Casey's prose need to be termed 'artificial' because it is not an exact recording of what can be heard in the streets of the capital of Ireland (in any case verbal inventiveness can be greater there than perhaps anywhere else in the world). No play can afford to offer an accurate replica of actual speech, except perhaps, but with a very different purpose, a comedy such as Ionesco's *The Bald Soprano*. No work of literature which presents people in a state of poetic, sentimental or other intoxication can depend entirely on ordinary speech—especially when seen as part of the tradition of literature in Ireland, where a stylised type of discourse was used, even by illiterate people, long before Lady Gregory or John Millington Synge. (It is already to be found, nearly a century earlier, in the novels of Maria Edgeworth, 1767–1849.)

Following the order used previously (characters, structure, language and style), we may consider the following: (*a*) the complaint that there is no 'central' character and too many useless minor ones; (*b*) quoting P.S. O'Hegarty, the assertion that 'the play has practically no plot', and that it shows no unity of design, structurally as well as stylistically.

The play is primarily concerned with men and women rather than with ideas or politics; it is about people's attitudes in a particular state of poverty, in particular conditions of war and terror, not about psychology irrespective of class and time. For this reason, O'Casey could not concentrate on one figure or on one point of view, but wished to show several diverse and divergent attitudes under the pressure of a period of troubles. He does not shirk from studying the contradictions within one person—and Davoren is a good example of this. At the same time, other characters provide effective contrast.

Davoren is the remorseful betrayer of his own ideals and love who is ultimately saved by compassion, the St Peter of the play, with whom he shares the triple denial before 'the village cock hath thrice done salutation to the morn' (p.110)—if it is permissible to ally the Bible with a purposely misquoted line from Shakespeare. Davoren lies to Minnie about his real nature (p.92), and about his acquaintance with Maguire:

> MINNIE: Did you know him, Mr Davoren?
> DAVOREN: Yes—no, no; I didn't know him, . . . Minnie.
> MINNIE: I wonder is it the Maguire that does be with Mr Shields?
> DAVOREN: Oh no, not at all, it couldn't be. (p.102)

He denies his fellow men: 'Damn the people! They live in the abyss, the poet lives on the mountain-top' (p.107). But he will not dare to deny his nationality completely:

AUX.: You're not an Irishman, are you?
DAVOREN: I—I—I was born in Ireland. (p.123)

And he will recognise his responsibility for Minnie's death, and the injustice and the pity of it. He graduates from shadow to existence.

The same cannot be said for Seumas, who does not show any more sympathy for the girl than he had for Maguire (p.106) and bluntly remarks: 'Is it my fault; am I to blame? . . . She did it off her own bat—we didn't ask her to do it' (p.129), and who makes no connection between the misfortunes of others and his own self, attributing evil to some vague, inescapable cause: 'I knew something ud come of the tappin' on the wall' (p.130). He has lost his opportunity of reaching consciousness and is condemned to live the rest of his life in lack of understanding and total blindness.

As for Minnie, she is a foil to both men, to Seumas's egotism but also to Davoren's cloudy idealism, a realist by necessity in front of the useless dreamer, as well as an unexpected heroine as opposed to the coward:

SEUMAS: I wouldn't care to have me life dependin' on brave little Minnie Powell—she wouldn't sacrifice a jazz dance to save it. (p.109)

Seumas had prophesied with his usual insight and in a wonderful instance of dramatic irony. He does not even have the decency—or the capacity—to recognise that he was wrong.

The three 'central' characters are essential to the unfolding of the fundamental theme of the play: that appearances differ from reality. They are not, however, sufficient to show why tenement-dwellers could not live up to the ideal that their leaders wished to impose on them—their economic conditions and the state of stupor they induced, their muddle-headedness about Ireland's heroic past, present and future, their general ignorance, their slavish habits, their fear, their having to resort to all kinds of drugs to forget the grimness of everyday life. For this reason minor characters, each contributing something to the general truth and by no means 'irrelevant', are introduced.

We now turn to the question of the play structure. *The Shadow of a Gunman* can be described as having no plot solely if the only perspective applied to the concept of the plot is bound to the set, unchangeable tradition based on a given time-pattern and progressing from *protasis* (introduction) to catastrophe or dénouement through *epitasis* (working up) and *catastasis* (counterturn). But a plot in space with a grouping of characters rather than a march of events is just as 'legitimate', as is what Robert Hogan calls the 'Chekhovian structure', which departs from the conventional single-action one by having 'an exterior action

. . . and a number of interior actions or plots which exemplify straightforwardly and ironically the major theme'.* It is towards this kind of form that O'Casey is undoubtedly feeling his way experimentally in the 'Dublin trilogy'.

The 'Dublin trilogy' has to be mentioned again at this point because a full appreciation of O'Casey's structural method should perhaps take into consideration the fact that *The Shadow of a Gunman* is only one-third, one movement so to speak, of a larger work which can usefully be studied as a whole. Both the critics David Krause and Ronald Ayling have done so, although they differ in the order they choose. Krause, in *Sean O'Casey: the Man and His Work*, takes the cycle in the order of composition of the plays, each of which has the same theme of probing into the illusions of heroism in a pacifist mood, the same setting (lower-life Dublin) and an action 'built around an ever-expanding radius of involvement. In the first play the conflict arises when a poet and a pedlar inadvertently become involved in the war; in the second play a whole family is caught in the crossfire of the battle; and in the third play all the people in the tenements are trapped by the war that now covers the whole city which is in flames at the end of the play.'† Ronald Ayling prefers the chronological order of subject-matter, in which *The Plough and the Stars* comes first, *The Shadow of a Gunman* second, and *Juno and the Paycock* third, but he also acknowledges the value of the cyclical vision which allows us to apprehend the plays' epic scale, their overall tragic view of life as well as their 'rebellion against the absurdly romanticised approach to history characteristic of the nineteenth-century theatre' (something very much in the line of George Bernard Shaw) and to see how they add up to 'a panoramic view of a country in a state of crisis'.**

Even if we consider *The Shadow of a Gunman* as self-contained and complete in itself, however, we can find in it strong arguments to counter the accusation that its various parts are unrelated, and that there is a lack of unity. On the contrary, the author's aim of exhibiting the conditions of war, tension and terror, and the reactions of a variety of people to such circumstances justifies his episodical method of presentation, his discursive and contrapuntal pattern. He avoids the pitfall of slackness by the rigour with which he uses strict counterbalancing elements—unity of place (which means that a good part of the action must occur off-stage) and unity of time. As regards the latter, even in as far as Maguire's short journey into death is concerned, he does not manage worse than Corneille who, in

* *The Experiments of Sean O'Casey*, p.28.

† David Krause, *Sean O'Casey: the Man and his Work*, Macmillan, New York, 1960.

** 'Sean O'Casey's Dublin Trilogy', *Sean O'Casey: a collection of Critical Essays*, ed. Thomas Kilroy, Prentice Hall, Englewood Cliffs, 1975, pp.77–89.

Le Cid, makes Rodrigue go away, fight and win a battle and come back to the court within a few hours. As witness to O'Casey's skill in handling plot, his selection of pregnant moments and the intensity of his handling of the essential episode in the play—the raid—are truly to be admired.

The diverse nature of the stylistic aspects of the play can also be explained in terms of its central theme. It would be absurd to attempt to treat all the characters in *The Shadow of a Gunman* as if they were all mouth-pieces of the author and he were using them merely as interchangeable instruments for the playing of his tuneful findings. The 'doers', the truly brave characters, hardly talk at all (this is the case with Maguire), or show an obvious reticence to express themselves (which is the case with Minnie, whose language is consistently unaffected and plain). Indeed they are not articulate enough, with the tragic result (consciously engineered by O'Casey) that their 'message'—the only sensible one—remains unspoken. The characters who pretend to be brave—Gallogher, Owens, Grigson, Shields, Davoren—on the other hand, flood the play with a cataract of words.

There are in each category individual differences due to education, mood, interests, activity, sex, personality and religion, but the patterns are similar. Both Davoren and Shields resort to refrain, one poetic ('Pain, pain, pain, ever, for ever!') the other mock-patriotic ('Oh, Kathleen ni Houlihan, your way's a thorny way'). Both Owens and Grigson (who belong to two different religious persuasions and two different political chapels, one a republican separatist, the other a unionist faithful to the King) use songs whose mediocrity and exaggeration underline their similarity as useless braggarts and stupid extremists of the tongue. All of them refer to *idées reçues*, hackneyed expressions of received half-truths, pompous inanities and images more colourful than meaningful, to cover their void and fear, their absence of personal opinion and their refusal to face reality. Even Seumas, critical though he is of patriotic and other clichés, uses them in his general complaints about the state of his unfortunate country or in the voicing of his superstitious fears. As for Donal Davoren, also a pretender but undergoing a more intense experience than his fellow blatherers, it is only at the very end of the play that his abandonment of Romantic literature for the sounder cadences of the Bible and the plain admission of his being a 'poltroon' reveals the possibility of his salvation.

The achievement of Sean O'Casey

Contrasting his own semi-hostile attitude to the text of *The Shadow of a Gunman* and his amazement at the play's effectiveness on the boards,

Robert Hogan came to the conclusion: 'A play may be drama and it may be literature, one or both. *The Gunman* is excellent drama.'*

Undoubtedly O'Casey's first play—and also, perhaps, his subsequent works—must be seen and heard in order properly to catch its most striking qualities: the contrast between the drabness of the setting and the floods of verbal imagination, or between the dullness and lack of taste of the other characters' dress and Minnie's natural elegance and prettiness; the rhythm, not only of the comings and goings but of the spoken word and accent which reveal their idiomatic raciness to the ear only (phonetic spellings are always poor renderings, and not only with O'Casey: think of George Bernard Shaw and his *Pygmalion*.) One also has to hear the music and the songs as well as the offstage sounds which are used so extensively: mysterious tappings, throbbing motor-engines, the tramping of heavy feet, the crash of glass and doors being beaten with rifle-butts, explosions of bursting bombs, followed by fierce and rapid revolver fire.

But the written text is not without its charm, its interest and its value. The stage directions are sufficiently detailed and telling to let the reader know or imagine the essentials and even the particulars of setting, characters and off-stage events. The dialogue, in spite of the slight difficulty brought about by the spelling, is catching and easy to follow. There is life, talk, colour, fun, pathos, suspense, and a style carried along by rhythm, alliteration and a continuing surge of metaphor.

The O'Casey who wrote *The Shadow of a Gunman* is not fundamentally different from the brilliant and moving author of the *Autobiographies*. Both works belong squarely within the realm of literature.

* *The Experiments of Sean O'Casey*, p.36.

Part 4

Hints for study

General points

The Shadow of a Gunman as part of a trilogy

(*a*) Sum up the similarities and differences between the three plays of the 'Dublin trilogy' (*The Shadow of a Gunman*; *Juno and the Paycock*; *The Plough and the Stars*), giving due consideration to the following:

Period concerned
Time (*The Shadow of a Gunman* covers one day; how long does each of the other plays cover?)
Width of experience
Human types; comic
Stage props and various dramatic devices (for instance, make a comparison of the dramatic effectiveness and impact between the bag containing bombs in *The Shadow of a Gunman*; the legacy in *Juno and the Paycock*; and the intercepted letter in *The Plough and the Stars*)
Do you agree that, apart from the unity of setting (Dublin) and of time (the period 1916 to independence) the main link between the three plays is the similarity of theme, that is, the effect of the Irish struggle on the innocent, and its nature as seen through their eyes?
Do you find a difference of mood between the plays? a progress in characterisation? in political thought?

(*b*) Reflect on the following quotation from Ronald Ayling's 'Sean O'Casey's Dublin Trilogy':*

> In O'Casey, as in Shakespeare's history plays [the reference is to *Richard II*, *Henry IV* (two parts), *Richard III*] certain recurrent themes are uppermost: the inter-action of public and private drama, the horror of civil strife and anarchy in the state, and, likewise in both, a continuing debate on the ambiguous demands of justice and order in society.

* In *Sean O'Casey: A Collection of Critical Essays*, ed. Thomas Kilroy, Prentice Hall, Englewood Cliffs, 1975, pp.77–89.

O'Casey and other playwrights

(*a*) O'Casey and Synge:
Comment upon the following statement by A.E. Malone:

> There is really no basis for comparison between O'Casey and Synge: Synge was a poet, with all the attributes of a poet; O'Casey is a photographic artist who retouches his films with an acid pencil to produce an effect of grotesque satire.*

(*b*) O'Casey and O'Neill:
If you are familiar with the works of the American playwright of Irish origin, Eugene O'Neill, you may find it useful to follow up the comparison Thomas Kilroy makes in his introduction to the O'Casey volume of the '20th Century Views' series:

> There is a more profitable comparison to be made between O'Casey and O'Neill. Both had early success and later neglect, and this was related to the efforts of both playwrights to impose form that would be acceptable in the modern theatre on material that was traditional and retrospective. Their careers in the theatre came to an end when human identity was being redefined in drama in terms that excluded —often violently, as in Beckett—the idea of consecutiveness implied by tradition . . . The virtues of both playwrights are histrionic, not literary. Both dramatized the pressures of modernity upon the units of traditional domesticity, upon the young imprisoned within hide-bound systems of an older generation or of older gods . . . Both respond, at times overenthusiastically, to contemporary experimentation . . . Finally, both flounder, at times, in seeking to go beyond the limits of their control of the language.†

(*c*) Other comparisons:
Bertold Brecht
Brendan Behan [*The Hostage*]

Nature and contents of *The Shadow of a Gunman*

(*a*) '*The Shadow of a Gunman* is that parody of tragedy called melodrama' (A.E. Malone).
(*b*) 'O'Casey's early plays represent the culmination of tragi-comedy' (Robert Hogan).
(*c*) 'Sean O'Casey is the most bookish of all Irish dramatists' (John Jordan).

* In *Sean O'Casey* (Modern Judgments Series), p.68.
† Thomas Kilroy: *Sean O'Casey* (20th Century Views); Prentice Hall, Englewood Cliffs, 1975, p.8.

(*d*) 'O'Casey's humour derives from the building-site at a lunch break or even a primary-school playground' (John Arden).
(*e*) 'The turbulent history through which Ireland had been living breaks into these tenements. As a direct action it is on the streets, and the people crowded in the houses react to it, in essential ways, as if it were an action beyond and outside them' (Raymond Williams).
(*f*) 'Mr Casey, your gift is characterisation' (Lady Gregory).

Detailed analyses: subject matter

The main theme: pretence

(*a*) Study which characters try to escape reality; what means do they use?
(*b*) When are those characters' fantasies funny? When do they cease to be so?
(*c*) Why was the title of the play changed from *On the Run* to *The Shadow of a Gunman*? What does the word 'shadow' convey to you?
(*d*) Notice how Minnie sees through Tommy Owens's pretence in Act I:

> TOMMY: ...remember that Tommy Owens only waits the call...
> MINNIE: Wouldn't that Tommy Owens give you the sick—only waitin' to hear the call! Ah, then it'll take all the brass bands in the country to blow the call before Tommy Owens ud hear it. (p.103)

How is it that she does not see through Davoren's?
(*e*) Study how, with each character, the language used underlines pretence. In the case of Davoren notice particularly his fondness for poetic diction (for instance, at the beginning of each act) which Seumas mocks in Act II, ('I don't know much about the pearly glint of the morning dew, or the damask sweetness of the rare wild rose, or the subtle greenness of the serpent's eye', pp.106–7). And, incidentally, is Seumas as critical of himself as he is of his companion?

Other themes

(*a*) *Poverty*:
Study some of the stage directions, for example, those describing Seumas's and Davoren's room (p.79) or those giving an account of Mrs Grigson's appearance and dress (p.113) to see how O'Casey manages to convey poverty through setting, costume and attitude. What do you find in the text proper that betrays the characters' economic difficulties?

Is the 'poverty' of the people only material poverty?

For help in answering the latter point, see Davoren's outburst at the beginning of Act II, or his estimate of Minnie a little later. You might also find some of O'Casey's later statements illuminating; for instance the following:

> Trade Unionism may give the worker a large dinnerplate—which, heaven knows, he badly needs—but it will never give him a broader mind, which he needs more badly still.

(*b*) *Religion*:
Show the impact of Catholicism on Seumas.
Show the impact of Protestantism on Grigson. (This includes the influence on their language. Also Grigson's use of the Bible.)
Show how both religions prove inadequate.
(*c*) *Politics*:
Study *The Shadow of a Gunman* in the light of O'Casey's pronouncement: 'Self realisation is more important than class consciousness.'

Characters

(*a*) *Minnie and the women*:
Comment on the following remark by Denis Johnston:

> O'Casey's interest in women is so profound that he might well be found guilty of Bretherton's famous charge against the whole Hibernian race—that of matriarchy.*

In answering this point, you could consider the following:

> O'CASEY: Women must be more courageous than the men. Courage doesn't consist in just firing a pistol and killing somebody, or taking the risk of firing a pistol and killing you. I wouldn't call that courage at all, I'd call it stupidity.
> DON ROSS [interviewer]: What does a woman's courage consist in?
> O'C: Fortitude – and patience – and understanding.
> D.R.: Is it true, then, that you think that women are more courageous than men.
> O'C: In life, yes: they're much more near to the earth than men are. Men are more idealistic, stupidly idealistic. They're not as realistic as women. The woman has to be nearer the earth than the men.
> D.R.: You like women then?
> O'C.: ... What on earth would we do without them?†

* *Sean O'Casey* (Modern Judgements Series), p.84.
† *The Sting and the Twinkle*, pp.92–3.

> The men in the play are intent on vanity or self-preservation; only the women show themselves capable of courage and charity like Minnie Powell's. The pathetic Mr Gallogher is under the wing of the immensely maternal Mrs Henderson . . . Grigson's drinking and boasting flourish at the expense of Mrs Grigson . . . In the face of danger and death, a moral paralysis affects the men, whereas the sympathies of women expand.*

> (O'Casey's) women who are the main victims of the war rise to become the main heroes . . . They are not the Romantic Ireland that idealized Kathleen ni Hoolihan of the beautiful green fields and the harp. They are not the sweet blushing colleens whose fabled existence is exalted in the guise of the Stage Irishwoman. They are the Ireland of tenacious mothers and wives, the women of the tenements—earthy, shrewd, laughing, suffering, brawling, independent women. O'Casey found them in the Dublin slums, but they have their counterparts in Synge's peasant woman, like Pegeen Mike in *The Playboy* and Mary Byrne in *The Tinker's Wedding*; in Joyce's Molly Bloom; in Yeats's Crazy Jane; in the eighteenth-century Brian Merriman's peasant girl of 'The Midnight Court'.†

Discuss the view of the playwright John O'Donovan (*b.* 1921) that 'Minnie is not a flesh and blood girl',** that she is too good and respectable and does not stand up to Rosie Redmond (in *The Plough and the Stars*).

Study Minnie Powell as 'an embodiment of an ideal fullness of life'. (W.A. Armstrong)

What do you think of her own remark that 'She's had to push her way through life without help from any one'? What light does it throw on her character?

'An ignorant little bitch that thinks of nothin' but jazz dances, fox-trots, picture theatres an' dress' is Seumas's assessment of Minnie. Davoren answers: 'Right glad I am that she thinks of dress, for she thinks of it in the right way, and makes herself a pleasant picture to the eye. Education has been wasted on many persons, teaching them to talk only, but leaving them with all their primitive instincts. Had poor Minnie received an education she would have been an artist. She is certainly a pretty girl. I'm sure she is a good girl, and I believe she is a brave girl' (pp.108–9). Do you agree with Davoren's assessment of Minnie?

* W.A. Armstrong, 'History, Autobiography, and *The Shadow of a Gunman*', *Modern Drama*, II, 4, February 1966, p.424.

† David Krause, *Sean O'Casey: the Man and his Work*.

** John O'Donovan, 'The Big Three', in *The World of Sean O'Casey*, ed. Sean McCann, Four Square Books, London, 1966, p.189.

(*b*) *Davoren*:

Just as Minnie has been described as anticipating a whole series of O'Casey's characters from Mary Boyle to Loreleen Maurthraun, Donal Davoren has been said to be a first sketch of Ayamonn (in *Red Roses for Me*). Do you agree with this idea?

Study Davoren as an embodiment of frustrated life.

Discuss John O'Donovan's view that 'It is easy enough to accept Davoren's estimate of himself as a poltroon, but not so easy to swallow him as the poet O'Casey tries to make of him . . . Donald Davoren doesn't convince the spectator that he is much more than poetic'.*

Do you think Davoren is a comic or a tragic character?

Do you find him sympathetic or the reverse?

Study the end of the play: is Davoren's 'epiphany' real self-revelation?

(*c*) *Seumas*:

Study Seumas as a prototype of Joxer (in *Juno and the Paycock*) and Fluther (in *The Plough and the Stars*).

Is he only an embodiment of life turned sour and superstitious?

O'Casey calls Seumas 'primitive'. Does he manage to show in what respect? How?

Study Seumas's egotism.

Study his misogyny. How do you account for it?

What are Seumas's functions in the play?

Detailed analyses: form

Characterisation

(*a*) Study how each character is presented; what—through the stage directions—we learn of his or her features, appearance, dress and so on; the way in which—through speech, mannerisms, attitudes, actions and reactions, the character and his or her role in the play develop.

(*b*) Contrast the stage directions concerning Mrs Grigson and then Mr Grigson (p.115). Show how the rest of the play is faithful to such indications.

(*c*) Which, in your opinion, are the characters that are used as the main unifying links in the play? Give examples to establish your point.

Structure

(*a*) *Divisions into scenes or episodes*:

Only the divisions into acts are indicated in *The Shadow of a Gunman*.

* Ibid, p.188.

Can you suggest, for each act, a further division into 'scenes' or, at any rate, 'episodes'?

In answering this question, would you agree with the following divisions?

ACT I (NOON AND AFTER):

1. pp.79–83 (from beginning to 'There's that fellow Maguire never turned up either,— he's almost too lazy to wash himself'): presents Davoren and Shields in their room and plants Maguire.
2. pp.83–4: Maguire's hurried visit; he leaves his bag behind.
3. pp.85–7 ('Another knock . . . Ah, go to hell!'): the squabble with the landlord.
4. pp.87–8 (to Minnie Powell's entrance): comment on the previous scene and revelation that Davoren is thought to be a gunman on the run.
5. pp.88–93 (to Tommy Owens's entrance): Minnie-Davoren scene: the shadow of a gunman again, and the first light of love.
6. pp.93–5 (to Mrs Henderson's entrance): the Tommy Owens scene.
7. pp.95–102 (to the Stop Press): Gallogher's letter to the Republican tribunal.
8. pp.102–3: news of the ambush and of Maguire's death.
9. pp.103–4 (to the end of the Act): resuming of the love-scene.

ACT II (NIGHT):

1. pp.105–13: Seumas's and Davoren's discussion is interrupted by the sound of a volley of shots. Terror grows.
2. pp.113–15: Mrs Grigson's complaint.
3. pp.115–20: Mr Grigson's scene; the raid comes nearer; he leaves with his wife.
4. pp.120–1: search for the letter to the tribunal; discovery of the contents of Maguire's bag; climax.
5. pp.121–2: climax continued: the raid is on the house, Minnie enters and takes the bag.
6. pp.122–6: the Auxiliaries' search: in Seumas's and Davoren's room; in the Grigsons'.
7. pp.126–8: Minnie's arrest offstage; the reactions to it.
8. pp.128–9: the Grigson & Shields scene.
9. pp.129–30: Minnie's death and funeral oration.

(*b*) *Dramatic peaks and turning points*:

Study the introduction and recurrence of the notion 'on the run' and Davoren's answer to it: 'on the run out'.

Follow the fortunes (or misfortunes) of the bag.

Comment on the Stop Press at the end of Act I; on the typing of Minnie's and Davoren's names on a slip of paper.

Study the various phases of the raid and its influence on the characters.

Language

(*a*) *As a means of characterisation; as a dramatic lever*:

Study Davoren's style, his fondness for adjectives (for instance, 'Shelley, the sensitive, high-minded, noble-hearted Shelley'), for aphorisms and antitheses, his rhetoric at large. What does it tell us about his character?

Study Seumas's speeches with their exclamations and parallel constructions.

Comment on Maguire's language: 'Keep your hair on; I just blew in ... Business, business. I'm going out to catch butterflies ... Can't be did ... if I waited till to-morrow all the butterflies might be dead.' (pp.83–4)

Seumas's stammering as a reflex and a means of delaying revelation.

Study the mock-legal vocabulary of the 'letter to the tribunal' scene (pp.98–101).

(*b*) *Dialect*:

Types and role of Irishisms in *The Shadow of a Gunman*.

In answering a question on dialect, you could consider the following: the instances of Irishisms in the play fall into five categories:

1. Phonetics:

Mute final consonant: in' (g); an', han', oul' (d); o' (f).

Modification of vowel or diphthong: meself (my); be (by); ud (would); sowl (soul); ardure (ardour); wan (one); ses (says).

2. Vocabulary:

At all, at all (p.80); the like of (p.81); argufyin' (p.85); gostherin' (p.85); Hooley (p.89); weeshy (p.89); dawny (p.90); mallavogin' (p.101); barrin' (p.109); sorra (p.114); goughers (p.116); gosterin' (p.128); etc.

Also some Gaelic words or phrases, like: 'Is truagh gan oidher 'na Vfarradh' (p.88); 'Sinn Fein Amhain' (p.101); 'traneen' (p.119).

3. Morphology:

'Can't be did' (p.84) and other instances of the popular confusion between preterite and past participle: 'what you seen' (p.94); 'hurted' (p.102); 'he has the poor woman's heart broke' (p.114); 'She had the house blew up' (p.127).

'Them' for 'these' (p.86 and elsewhere).

'It was *the* sorry day' (p.86).

'You was' (p.93) and other instances of a singular verbal form with a plural subject.

'More nor' for 'more than' (p.96).

'Childer' for 'children' (p.99).

'Yous' (p.201).

4. Syntax:

'There's the braces after breakin' = 'the braces have just broken' (p.83); also, 'they're after gettin' a whole lot of stuff' (p.127).

Extensive use of the progressive form: 'don't be tryin' to make a cod o' me' (p.83); 'I shouldn't be troublin' you' (p.89).

'It's meself that hopes you're feelin' well' (p.85); 'It's himself has them trained well' (p.103); 'If they do aself' (p.122).

Double negatives as in 'I don't come here to raise no argument' (p.85).

Use of the auxiliary 'do' with 'to be' as in 'Do you be all alone all the day?' (p.89); 'I do be on the watch every night' (p.121).

'He has a few drinks taken' (p.93) (the inversion is O'Casey's, own here, as it is to be found in the stage-directions); 'he has a sup taken' (pp.113–4).

Omission of the relative pronoun even if a subject: 'There's plenty of men can't sleep' (p.110).

Present participles with a personal pronoun used as a subject: 'The Angelus was ringin' out an' we sittin' at the table' (113); 'They had the poor man sittin' up in bed, an' he singin' a hymn . . . an' they all laughin' (p.125).

'Mr Grigson, is it?' (p.113); 'Mindin' me, is it?' (p.115).

'What's all the bother about?' says I . . . 'No back talk, says he.' (p.128).

5. Rhetoric:

Comparisons are numerous, as is often the case in Irish writing; for instance, 'You'll be as welcome as the flowers in May' (p.96); 'as decent an' honest an' quiet a man as you'd meet in a day's walk' (and see the earlier paragraph on the comedy of words, p.47). So are exaggerations. Many references are to Irish figures and notions and Irish phrases; for instance, 'Up with the Republic', 'Land of Saints and Scholars', and similar instances.

Most Irishisms are put in the mouths of ordinary Dubliners (rather than educated characters like Davoren); they therefore serve a purpose of characterisation and local colour or have a partly (or totally) comic function. But they are also part and parcel of the author's vision. Sean O'Casey himself was to remark: 'Like Joyce, it is only through an Irish scene that my imagination can weave a way'.*

* In *Blasts and Benedictions*, ed. Ronald Ayling, Macmillan, London, 1967, p.144.

Part 5

Suggestions for further reading

The text

The Shadow of a Gunman, a tragedy in 2 acts (first performed 12 April 1923, Abbey Theatre, Dublin). The text first appeared in print in *Two Plays*, Macmillan, London, 1925; reprinted in *Collected Plays*, Vol.1, Macmillan, London, 1949.

Other plays by Sean O'Casey

Cathleen Listens In (also *K*athleen), a (political) phantasy in 1 act (first performed 1 October 1923, Abbey Theatre, Dublin). First appearance in print: *Tulane Drama Review*, June 1961; reprinted in *Feathers from the Green Crow* (see below under 'Other Works by Sean O'Casey (Collected)'), 1962.

Juno and the Paycock, a tragedy in 3 acts (first performed 3 March 1924, Abbey Theatre, Dublin), *Two Plays*, Macmillan, London, 1925; *Collected Plays*, Vol.1, Macmillan, London, 1949. There was a film by Alfred Hitchcock in 1929 and a musical by Joseph Stein in 1959.

Nannie's Night Out, a comedy in 1 act (first performed 29 September 1924, Abbey Theatre, Dublin), *Feathers from the Green Crow* (see below), 1962.

The Plough and the Stars, a tragedy in 4 acts (first performed on 8 February 1926, Abbey Theatre, Dublin) Macmillan, London, 1926; *Collected Plays*, Vol.1, Macmillan, London, 1949. There was a John Ford film in 1937 and an opera by Elie Siegmeister (first entitled *Dublin Song*, 1963; revised, under O'Casey's original title, 1969).

The Silver Tassie (first performed 11 October 1929, Apollo Theatre, London), Macmillan, London, 1928; *Collected Plays*, Vol.2, Macmillan, London, 1949.

Within the Gates, a play of 4 scenes in a London Park (first performed 7 February, 1934, Royalty Theatre, London), Macmillan, London, 1933; *Collected Plays*, Vol.2, Macmillan, London, 1949.

A Pound on Demand, a sketch in 1 act (first performed in 1936, Darlington Grammar School, Durham), *Windfalls* (see below), 1934; *Collected Plays*, Vol. 1, Macmillan, London, 1949; *Five One-Act Plays*, Macmillan, London, 1958.

The End of the Beginning, a comedy in 1 act (first performed 8 February 1937, Abbey Theatre Dublin), publishing details as for *A Pound on Demand*, above.

The Star Turns Red (first performed 12 March 1940, Unity Theatre, London), Macmillan, London, 1940; *Collected Plays*, Vol.2, Macmillan, London, 1949.

Red Roses For Me (first performed 15 March 1943, Olympia Theatre, Dublin), Macmillan, London, 1942; *Collected Plays*, Vol. 3, Macmillan, London, 1951; *Three More Plays*, Macmillan, London, 1965 (a final, revised edition).

Purple Dust, a wayward comedy (first performed 16 December 1943, People's Theatre, Newcastle upon Tyne), London, Macmillan, 1940; *Collected Plays*, Vol.3, Macmillan, London, 1951; *The Genius of the Irish Theatre*, ed. Barnet, Berman & Burto, Mentor Books, New York, 1960 (a final, revised edition).

Oak Leaves and Lavender (first performed 13 May 1947, Lyric Theatre, Hammersmith), Macmillan, London, 1946; *Collected Plays*, Vol. 4, Macmillan, London, 1951.

Cock-A-Doodle Dandy, a fantasy drama in 3 scenes (first performed 10 December 1949, People's Theatre, Newcastle upon Tyne), Macmillan, London, 1949; *Collected Plays*, Vol.4, Macmillan, London, 1951.

Hall of Healing, a sincerious farce in 1 scene (first performed 7 May 1952, Yugoslav American Hall, New York), *Collected Plays*, Vol.3, Macmillan, London, 1951.

Bedtime Story, an Anatole burlesque in 1 act (first performed with *Hall of Healing*, above): Publication details as *Hall of Healing*.

Time To Go, a morality comedy in 1 act (first performed with *Hall of Healing* above), *Collected Plays*, Vol.4, Macmillan, London, 1951. (All the three plays above are also included in *Five One Act Plays*, Macmillan, London, 1958.)

The Bishop's Bonfire, a tragi-comedy in 3 acts (first performed 26 February 1955, Gaiety Theatre, Dublin), Macmillan, London, 1955.

The Drums of Father Ned, a mickrocosm of Ireland (first performed 25 April, Little Theatre, Lafayette, Indiana), Macmillan, London: St Martin's Press, New York, 1960.

Figuro in the Night (first performed 4 May 1962, Hafastra University Playhouse, New York).

The Moon Shines on Kynelamoe (first performed 30 October 1962, Theatre de Lys, New York).

Behind the Green Curtains (first performed 5 December 1962, University of Rochester, New York State), *Behind the Green Curtains, Figuro in the Night, The Moon Shines on Kylenamoe*, Macmillan, London; St Martin's Press, New York, 1961.

Other Works by Sean O'Casey (Collected)

Autobiographies (1939–54):
Inishfallen, Fare Thee Well, Macmillan, New York, 1949.
Mirror in My House, Macmillan, New York, 2 vols, 1956.
Autobiographies, Macmillan, London, 2 vols, 1963.
Autobiography, Pan Books, London, 6 vols, I and II, 1971; III and IV, 1972; V and VI, 1973.

Miscellaneous Collections:
Windfalls, Macmillan, London, 1934.
The Flying Wasp, Macmillan, London, 1937.
The Green Crow, George Braziller, New York, 1956.
Feathers from the Green Crow, ed. Robert Hogan, University of Missouri Press, Columbia, 1962.
Under a Colored Cap, Macmillan, London; St Martin's Press, New York, 1963.
Blasts and Benedictions, ed. Ronald Ayling, Macmillan, London; St Martin's Press, New York, 1967.
The Sting and the Twinkle. Conversations with Sean O'Casey, ed. E.H. Mikhail and John O'Riordan, Macmillan, London, 1974.
The Letters of Sean O'Casey, ed. David Krause, Macmillan, New York, Vol.1 (1910–41), 1975; Vol.2 (1942–54), 1980. Third volume in preparation.

Historical background

LYONS, F.S.L.: *Ireland Since the Famine*, Weidenfeld & Nicolson, London, 1971; Fontana (paperback), London, 1973.
FITZPATRICK, DAVID: *Politics and Irish Life 1913–1921*, Gill & Macmillan, Dublin, 1977.

Literary background

MERCIER, VIVIAN: *The Irish Comic Tradition*, Clarendon Press, Oxford, 1962.
TRUNINGER, ANNELISE: *Paddy and the Paycock*. A Study of the Stage-Irishman from Shakespeare to O'Casey, Francke, Berne, 1976.
ELLIS-FERMOR, UNA: *The Irish Dramatic Movement*, Methuen, London, 1939.

Bibliographies

AYLING, RONALD AND DURKAN, MICHAEL J.: *Sean O'Casey. A Bibliography*. Macmillan, London, 1978.

MIKHAIL, E.H.: *Sean O'Casey: A Bibliography of Criticism*, Macmillan, London, 1972.

Biographies and memoirs

KRAUSE, DAVID: *Sean O'Casey and His World*, Thames & Hudson, London, 1976.

FALLON, GABRIEL: *Sean O'Casey: The Man I Knew*, Routledge & Kegan Paul, London; Little, Brown, Boston and Toronto, 1965.

O'CASEY, EILEEN: *Sean*, Macmilan, London, 1971.

Studies

BENSTOCK, BERNARD: *Paycocks and Others. Sean O'Casey's World*, Gill & Macmillan, Dublin; Barnes and Noble, New York, 1976.

COWASJEE, SAROS: *O'Casey*, (Writers and Critics Series), Oliver & Boyd, Edinburgh and London, 1960.

GREAVES, C. DESMOND: *Sean O'Casey: Politics and Art*, Lawrence & Wishart, London, 1979.

HOGAN, ROBERT: *The Experiments of Sean O'Casey*, St Martin's Press, New York, 1960.

KRAUSE, DAVID: *Sean O'Casey: the Man and His Work*, Macmillan, New York, 1960; new edition, Collier Macmillan, London, 1975.

SMITH, B.L.: *O'Casey's Satiric Vision*, Kent State University Press, Ohio, 1978.

Articles

Collections:

AYLING, RONALD (ED.): *Sean O'Casey* (Modern Judgments Series), Macmillan, London, 1969.

KILROY, THOMAS (ED.): *Sean O'Casey: A Collection of Critical Essays*, Prentice Hall, Englewood Cliffs, 1975.

KRAUSE, DAVID AND LOWERY, ROBERT G. (EDS.): *Sean O'Casey, Centenary Essays* (Irish Literary Studies, 7), Colin Smythe, Gerrards Cross, 1980.

LOWERY, ROBERT G. (ED.): *Essays on Sean O'Casey's 'Autobiographies'*, Macmillan, London, 1981.

McCANN, SEAN (ED.): *The World of Sean O'Casey* (The New English Library), Four Square Books, London, 1966.

Journals:

ARMSTRONG, WILLIAM A.: 'History, Autobiography, and *The Shadow of a Gunman*', in *Modern Drama*, II, 4, February, 1960.

MURRAY, CHRISTOPHER (ED.): *Sean O'Casey: Roots and Branches*, special issue of *Irish University Review*, X, 1, Spring 1980.

RITCHIE, HARRY M.: 'The Influence of Melodrama on the Early Plays of Sean O'Casey', in *Modern Drama*, V, 2, September 1962.

ROLLINGS, RONALD G.: 'Form and Content in Sean O'Casey's Dublin Trilogy', in *Modern Drama*, VIII, 4, February 1960.

SCHRANK, BERNICE: '"You Needn't Say No More": Language and the Problems of Communication in Sean O'Casey's *The Shadow of a Gunman*', in *Irish University Review*, VIII, 1, Spring 1978.

The Sean O'Casey Review, ed. Robert G. Lowery, P.O. Box 333, Holbrook, New York.

The author of these notes

PATRICK RAFROIDI was educated at the Sorbonne. Agrégé d'anglais, Docteur-ès-lettres, he has taught in Paris, Rouen, Strasbourg, Bloomington and at the University of Lille of which he is Honorary Vice-Chancellor and where he holds the Chair of Contemporary English and Anglo-Irish Literature. From 1976 to 1979 he was Chairman of the International Association for the Study of Anglo-Irish Literature. His publications include *Irish Literature in English: the Romantic Period, 1789–1850* (1980), and he is at present working on a sequel concerning the years 1850–1921. He has also written York Notes on James Joyce's *Dubliners*. He is the founder and chief editor of the yearly journal *Etudes Irlandaises*. He completed this study of *The Shadow of a Gunman* while a Visiting Fellow at the Humanities Research Centre of the Australian National University in Canberra. He has since been appointed Director of the French Institute in London.